NINETY YEARS
COUNTRY

Harold Meeks

Harold Meeks
23/2/96

King's Music
1993

King's Music
Redcroft, Bank's End, Wyton, Huntingdon, Cambs PE17 2AA

© Harold Meeks 1993

ISBN 1 871775 03 5

All rights reserved. No part of this publication may be reproduced, stored in a retrieval system, or transmitted in any form or by any means, electronic, mechanical, photocopying, recording or otherwise, without the prior permission of King's Music.

Typeset by King's Music
Printed by Stanwick Print Services Limited

FOREWORD

Several years ago a very dear friend of mine, Sir Godfrey Nicholson, was distraught with grief at the death of his beloved wife, and his four daughters urged him to write his memoirs for them and their children. It was a wonderful therapy, and a fascinating personal account of a full life. It was never intended for publication, nor has it been; but it brought home to me as an historian how important it is that as many people as possible should write their autobiography.

Also, for reasons that puzzle me, the British are far less interested in local history than other nations, particularly the Americans. One of the charms of my village, Great Gransden, is that it has existed for centuries and nothing in particular has happened until the Second World War brought the British, Canadian and American bomber crews. But it is England, where generations have lived, worked, been happy, suffered sadnesses and tragedies, and are buried in the sleepy churchyard. I only wish we knew more about them.

It was therefore with particular joy that I found out about Harold Meeks's memoirs, marvellously edited by Dora Tack, which I have enjoyed so much. It is very much a countryman's book, written simply and clearly, and often reminds me – as in the sad account of the cutting down of Papworth Wood – of what we have lost, thanks to 'progress'. But it is wonderfully evocative, and will give immense pleasure to everyone who loves our part of England and wants to know more about it.

Sir Robert Rhodes James

The photograph opposite shows some of the tools that Harold has used on contract work during his lifetime:–

Spades for land draining, hoes for all of the different sized pipes. A tiling hook and foot iron for digging.

Spades for ditching, hedge cutting tools for trimming and hedge laying.

Axes, saws, wedges and hammers for tree felling.

Thatching tools – rakes, shears and measuring tape.

Hay knives and needles for hay pressing.

Sugar beet hoes, used when crawling on hands and knees when setting out the beet. Knives for cutting off the beet tops.

Forks for potato digging.

Old lantern for going round the farm at night.

Two-tined forks for using with straw, sheaves and hay. (When he was stacking he always used a fork.)

Four-tined fork (muck fork) used for forking manure.

Scythe and gathering rake for mowing corn and tying it up into sheaves.

Swob and hook for cutting Maple-peas and tares.

In the foreground is some of his 'pest destruction' equipment:–

12-bore shot-guns, rat traps, rat snares, ferret box, mole traps and rabbit snares. Most of these items are still being used by Harold at the age of the ninety-two.

To represent his sporting interests he is holding cricket bat and pads and his boxing gloves; in his younger days he was very fond of both of these sports.

Contents

Foreword by Sir Robert Rhodes James
Preface by Dora Tack
Introduction: my family   1
1. Childhood   9
2. Hard Working Days   47
3. Reflections   121

Illustrations

Walter Meeks aged 21 (Harold's father).	5
Harold with his nephew Haddon Currington.	5
'Charlie' Meeks (Harold's brother).	6
Arthur Meeks.	6
Walter Meeks 'Buller'.	7
Jessie Meeks.	7
Yelling Night School, 1911.	8
Yelling School, Division 1, 1908.	43
Men of the Duke of Bedford's Regiment.	44
Mary-Ann and Robert Wheal.	45
Yelling Mill, 1900.	45
Croxton Saw Mill in the 1920s.	46
Goog Thody holding a horse.	46
Dry Close, 1928.	83
Harvest on Mr Rampley's land, 1932.	83
Yelling cricket team, 1924.	84
Yelling cricket team, 1929.	85
Working for the British Insulated Cables Co., 1929.	86
Hilda's mother and grandmother, 1880.	117
Harold and Hilda's wedding, 26th March 1924.	117
Reg Meek's wedding, 20th March 1943.	118
High Hayden Farm, Yelling.	118
Harold and son, 1927.	119
Raymond, 1929.	119
Harold and Ray, 1960.	119
Harold and Hilda, 1956.	120
Ray, Hilda and Harold, 1957.	120

Colour illustrations

Harold, Ray and pigeons, Papworth, 1986.
Harold, Ray and rabbits, Hamerton, 1987.
Harold, Ray and rats, 1987.
William Topham, Harold and fox.
Harold and Ray outside Gremblin Grange, 1987.
Harold in his flower garden, 1987.

PREFACE

The unexpected well-wrapped package dropped with a plop on my front door mat. The post-mark was local. I opened it and found several pages of closely written manuscript, and a letter from Harold Meeks, aged 90 – a friend of my late husband from the 1950s. He had read my book *From Bombs to Buckets* and enjoyed it, and wrote "I am sending you the first pages of my book. Please sort it out and send it to your publisher." I had never done anything like this before.

Harold had written as he remembered, in any order of occurrence. Using the skills I had learnt at the General Electric Company, Hammersmith, in the 1930's, I typed each episode, numbering each paragraph as I proceeded. I sent these typed sheets to Harold, asking him to to write the approximate date in the margin and to answer my queries, quoting the paragraph number. This he did, and returned the typed sheets to me. We repeated this procedure many times over a period of several weeks until his manuscript was complete.

Then I cut each paragraph separately, and sitting on the floor I spread all the piles of similar dates around me, arranging them in date order. Taking each pile, I read and re-arranged the text to best effect, then retyped the whole book in the new order – and posted it off to the Bartletts. Elaine phoned to say that it had been accepted and asked, "Did you enjoy editing the book?" So that's what I did: I never knew until she told me!

Dora Tack

The author would like to thank Miss Elaine Donaldson, Mr Reg Cawthorne, Miss Joan Fairy, Mrs Richard Hart, Mr Ronald Hedge, Mrs Walter Meeks, Mr Frank Reed, Mrs Joan Smith, Mr Bernard Swales and Mr Sykes for lending photographs and Mr Gerald Papworth for taking some specially for this book.

INTRODUCTION: MY FAMILY

I was born at Yelling, a village in Huntingdonshire, on 17 January 1901, at New Zealand (the west end of Yelling, not the other side of the world!) In 1921 my parents and family moved into Friends Farm at the other end of the village, which my father farmed for 16 years. I married Miss Hilda Topham who lived at the Hand in Hand public house in Toseland, which her mother and father kept for 30 years. We were married on 26 March 1924 and took over half of the house from Hilda's mother and father. There was plenty of space as there were nine rooms in the house. That was where my wife had been born and it was where our son Raymond was born. Later we moved to Lodge Farm and, after three and a half years there, to a cottage in the village.

Now, in 1992, Raymond and I are living along the Toseland to St Neots road. The name of the house is Gremblin Grange - it used to be two cottages called Hollow Farm Cottages. During the wartime, I rented one cottage to a Flight Sergeant from Graveley Airfield, who worked on the plane G for George and G for Grem(b)lin. His wife and daughter lived there too, during the war and for a time afterwards. The Flight Sergeant named the cottage Gremblin Grange for luck, as he said all the times that the plane had been on bombing raids, it had always returned without a scratch. So that was how our house got its name. Since then, the two cottages have been made into one and that is how it is today.

My father used to tell me about his brother, Charles, who was employed as page-boy, rising to butler, by the Newton family. My grandfather was gamekeeper to the Croxton Estate, living at Depden House, which stood at the Yelling end of the plantation on Mr Gordon Ashcroft's farm. I remember the plantation being planted by Mr Walter Peak in 1910. His two sons, Bill and Herbert, and I often paid him a visit after school to watch him planting the trees. Later, my father planted the first lot of trees on the Croxton fruit farm.

My father and mother were Walter and Catherine Meeks and there was a large family – seven boys and one girl. The boys were Charles, William, Arthur, Walter (always known as 'Buller'), Harold, Stanley and Reginald. The girl's name was Violet.

The oldest boy, Charles, joined the Nottingham City Police in 1912, and in 1914 he volunteered for the Army. In a very short time, he was promoted to Sergeant Rough-Riding Instructor in the Royal Field Artillery. While serving in France, he was Sergeant on Number One Gun, the eighteen pounders. During one battle, they lost several horses, which were replaced by Canadian wild horses. One day, one of these horses broke away and the Officer in Charge said, "Is there any man who will volunteer to catch that horse?" My brother Charles said, "Yes, I will." He ran along beside the horse and grabbed its bridle. At that moment, the horse stood up on its hind legs and fought him with its front feet, which hit my brother. The iron shoes made a terrible mess of his face and knocked several of his teeth out.

After a few days in hospital, he was sent home and had his wounds attended to by Dr Harrison of St Neots, who came every day for several weeks. Dr Harrison said, "It would have killed nine men out of ten and it is only being a strong man, Charlie, that has pulled you through."

Now about my brother William. One very hot day in July, when he was about 11 years old, he came out of school at 12 o'clock and, on his way home from school, he went bathing in a pond near Yelling Chapel. The pond was covered by trees, so the water was very cold and he caught a chill. He died in less than 24 hours.

Next was my brother Arthur. He also served in the Royal Field Artillery during the First World War. He spent quite a long time in France. One morning we had a Field Card to say he was missing. He lost all his mates while he was on the run. He found my brother Charlie and stayed with him until he was found after the war.

My brother Arthur ran Yelling Chapel for over 50 years and his wife was organist for the same number of years. He was also head of the Managers of Yelling School, Chairman of Yelling and Toseland Council, sat on the Rural District Council and also the War Executive Committee; he was also a farm worker.

Then there was my brother Buller; he also served in the Army during the First World War. He was a corporal in the Royal West Kent Regiment and he also did long service in France. While he was at home on leave, "Jerry" broke through and wiped all his lot out, so when he returned all his mates had gone. During the Second World War, he was on the Police Reserve at Caxton, Cambridgeshire. He worked for Collings Brothers at Abbotsley until he retired.

The next son was Harold - me. But you can read all about me in this book!

Next was my brother Stanley. He worked at home on the farm, and he also worked for Mr Mailer at Hill Farm, Papworth St Agnes. He came with Charlie, Buller and me to work on the British Insulated Cables. While we were working at Potters Bar, Stan was offered a job as gardener at Clare Hall Sanatorium, South Mimms. He became the Head Gardener and worked there for over 30 years until he retired. Stan was very fond of dancing. When he went out dancing, he would arrive home in the early hours of the morning. If we said to him, "You were out late last night," he would reply, "Yes, I was sitting around the fire with some Gypsies for an hour or two!" Nothing worried Stan! He was also an excellent shot with a catapult. He filled his pockets with small potatoes and went round houses, shining his torch under the eaves, looking for roosting sparrows. He didn't miss very often. Using potatoes did not damage the property.

My brother Reginald worked at home on the farm too. He did all the tractor work, milking the cows, etc. When my father retired and left the farm, Reg made his home with my brother Arthur. Reg went tractor driving for the War Agricultural Committee. Then, as I was contracting for War-Ag work, I got Reg off the Committee to work for me, which he did for several years. Then Reg went on to lorry driving, taking vegetables (sprouts, etc.) to London each night. From that job, he went on to lorry driving for Mr Wrycroft, Builders. When Mr Wrycroft finished, he went to work for the Eastern Electricity Board until he retired.

Then there was my sister, Violet. She worked for Miss Susannah Hedge at her shop in Yelling, and also helped my mother in the house. We were a large family, so Mother was glad of her help and she found plenty to do. She married Arthur Currington, who was a Steam Cultivator Engine driver and a steam-roller driver. Later on, he worked with me on the British Insulated Cables. One evening, on our way home from Renhold, near Bedford, where we had been working, we hit a ten-ton lorry head on, and Arthur was killed instantly. Years later, their only son, Haddon, and my son Ray had visited me in Huntingdon Hospital and were on their way home when they had an accident in Offord, and Haddon was killed. So, I was with my sister's husband when he was killed, and my son Ray was with my sister's son when he was killed – 50 years later than his father.

Harold with his nephew Haddon Currington. The photograph was taken by Mr Bert Sandiver in the back garden of his sister's home in 1920. Harold and Bert were working for Mr Wrycroft of St Neots, building the four houses opposite.

Walter Meeks aged 21 (Harold's father).

'Charlie' Meeks (Harold's brother). A sergeant, rough-riding instructor in the Royal Field Artillery.

Arthur Meeks. Also in the Royal Field Artillery.

Walter Meeks 'Buller'. Served in France as a corporal in the Royal West Kent Regiment.

Jessie Meeks. Harold's uncle. He was in the 7th Bedfordshire Regiment and lost his right leg in France in 1916. He was given a Military Medal for bravery on the field.

Yelling Night School – 1911

The photograph was taken by The Head School Master, Mr E.J. Quick, in Yelling school room in paraffin lamplight.

Back row, from left to right William Peak, Walter Cullip, George Howlett, Harry Franklin, Arthur Meeks (*brother*), Percy Norman, Edward Howlett
Third row Charles Meeks (*brother*), Thomas Hedge, James Meeks (*uncle*), William Currington (Bib), Sidney Currington, Thomas Reed, Ben Reed, Walter Currington (Phip)
Second row Walter Meeks (Buller) (*brother*), William Currington (Otty), Charlie Norman, James Norman
Front row David Howlett, Jessie Meeks (*uncle*), Arthur Currington (*brother-in-law*)

1. CHILDHOOD

I started to go to school at Yelling when I was three years old. The Schoolmaster and Schoolmistress were Mr and Mrs E. J. Quick and the school teacher was Miss Edith Howlett. Mrs Quick was in the Infants' Room, Mr Quick and Miss Howlett in the big room. Mr Quick was a good master, very strict, and he didn't hesitate about using his cane! I remember once he called me out in front of the class for talking and gave me two strokes with the cane. On my way back to my desk, I said, "I'll tell my dad," and he came and grabbed hold of me, laid me across his knee and gave me three more strokes on the behind. When I got home, there was no need to tell my dad, because my brothers had already told him. Then I had another good hiding from my father with his leather belt. I did not try that silly trick any more.

When I first started school, my mother bought me a new overcoat. On a lovely sunny afternoon, when it was quite hot, I wanted to wear my new coat, but my mother wouldn't let me put it on. On the way to school, I cried all the way, until we got down into the village and my grandmother heard me crying. She asked my sister what was the matter, and my sister told her. Then my grandmother got hold of me and took me into her house and put me on the stairs. She got her stick and said, "One sound from you and you will get this." She kept me on the stairs all the afternoon and I was afraid to make a sound. When my brothers and sister came out of school, she fetched me off the stairs and gave me a rock cake, saying, "That is for being a good boy."

When I was four years old, I went with my mother to Croxton Church to the wedding of Sir Douglas and Lady Newton, but we could not get into the church. We stood outside and waited until they came out. The fly (one-horsed carriage) was waiting outside the church for them and they got up into the seat, which was quite high. They were pulled along from the church, round through Croxton village, along the A45 and down to the big house, by Croxton Cricket Team – all in white. Then we all sat down to lunch.

When I was five years old and my playmate Victor Norman was the same age, we were playing near the pond close to our homes. The pond was very deep. Victor opened the gate and went down the steps where the people went to dip out buckets of water, and he fell in. I stood and watched him come to the surface once, twice, then no more. At that moment Mr Conington from Godmanchester, who came round for orders for groceries on Mondays and delivered them on Tuesdays, came round the corner. I told him that Victor Norman had fallen in the pond. He laid down his book and jumped in the pond, fully clothed, to bring Norman out. But it was too late. I had lost my playmate.

When I was very young, there was a farmer named Joey Ashcroft who farmed High Hayden Farm. He had a large copper in which he boiled wheat which, when cooked, made frumenty, a nourishing milky food. He boiled it for the people in Yelling and the women walked up the fields to High Hayden with their basins, which he filled for their dinner. When he died, he left quite a bit of money - enough to buy one hundredweight of coal for each house in the village each year. It was delivered by Jim Norman, the coalman, every Christmas. When he arrived with the coal at our house, he would say," Gift coal today, mate." That went on for many years.

During my school days, a lot of tradesmen came into the village of Yelling:

Butchers Bartlett and Sam Abraham from St Neots. They called three times a week. We also had a butcher, Mr Fred Stocker living in the village.

Bakers Abraham from St Neots, Bradley from Great Paxton and Joe Skimpton from Whitehall, who worked for Mr Ashcroft.

Fishmongers Wrens from St Neots and John Garret from Croxton.

Sweets and Greengrocery Wiles from Eaton Socon and Petchy from Eynesbury.

Coalman Jim Norman, who lived in the village, Gale from Offord and Meggy Ratcliffe, who worked for Jordan and Addington.

Groceries Mr Conington from Godmanchester, Freeman from St Neots, International from St Neots and Consumers from St Neots.

Shops in the village: There were three shops, which were kept by Miss Hedge, Mr and Mrs Tom Wood and Mr John Tack. Ben Reed also sold various items. His house was on the road from Fred Stocker's butcher's shop. He sold paraffin, balls of whitening and also treacle dabs at four for a penny! There was also a Post Office.

Public House The White Swan.

Carpenters, wheelwrights and undertakers Joseph Ellwood, David Woods and David Howlett.

Shoe-makers Neremiah Reed (known as 'Nere') and Richard King.

Harness makers Billy Fields and Willy Wyne.

Blacksmith Mr Lewis.

Chimney sweep Joe Reed.

There also used to be people coming round the villages shouting "Rags, bones or rabbit skins!"

Now, in 1990, there is nothing! No tradesmen living in the village and nobody calling and delivering.

During my school days, a very big family of gypsies, the Bird family, sometimes came into the village. There was an old man, Tommy Bird, and his wife, and 20 to 30 children, grand-children, etc, all trailing along behind the old man and woman in a stream nearly a mile long. There were also five or six scissor grinders and about 20 prams, and when they entered the village, the men and women all came out of their houses to watch them come in. One evening, as they were coming into the village, the old man and woman were rowing. The old man was kicking the prams over into the ditch. The old woman shouted, "Clear the way, ladies and gentlemen, here comes the devil a-flying!" When they reached their destination in the bridle road that leads to Graveley, they got their fires going. Then the old man went to the manure heap in Mr Farr's farmyard, where Mr Farr buried all his dead hens, pigs or calves. He stuck his hand down in the heap and then looked at his fingers. If he had found one (a body), he would say, "I like them when they are 'meller' [mellow]!"

In 1910, I stood outside our house, looking at Haley's Comet. There were a lot of people watching it and we could see it quite clearly, with its long tail. I was told that if its tail touched the ground, the world would come to an end. Its position in the sky was about North-North-East.

I often think about how things have changed since I was a boy. We would sit in the house on winter evenings with an oil lamp on the table. If you wanted to go anywhere else in the house, you would carry a candlestick with a lighted candle in it. On the 5th of November, Guy Fawkes Day, we would buy a 'halfpenny worth of matches' (they were three boxes for a halfpenny).

On summer evenings, us kids would play Hopscotch, or Spin Tops, or Blow Bubbles or just sit on the road outside our houses and play marbles or noughts and crosses or sticks and stones without being disturbed. We also played Tip Taps, which I think needs the some explanation:

A Tip-tap is a piece of wood about six inches long, sharpened to a point at each end. You hit it with a stick to make the tip-tap jump up in the air, and then swing the stick to see how far you can hit it. There are two teams. Two circles are chalked on the road, the outer circle with a diameter of two or three yards, the inner circle of about 12 inches. The Tip-tap is thrown in from outside the outer ring by the opposing team. If it lands in the little circle, you get one hit, if within the larger circle, you get two. The side which hits the tip-tap furthest wins.

The women from the village would be coming past to go to the allotments to meet their husbands, who had just left their work in the fields. They were bringing them some food and a can of tea, so that they could do some work in their allotments when they had finished their tea. When they decided that they had had enough for one day, we would see them coming home with their baskets full of new potatoes, green beans, broad beans, etc. Almost every householder in the village had a piece of land in the allotments – but today that is a thing of the past.

An old chap used to come round with a truck selling windmills. He used to shout, "Two jam jars for one windmill!" Us kids would go round the houses, knocking on doors to ask, "Have you got any jam jars, please?"

To pass the winter's evenings away, we played draughts, snakes and ladders, ludo, dominoes, steeplechase, or cards. We would often have dictation, which I liked very much. One would call out the words while the others wrote them down. When we had all finished, we would check them all to see who had got the most mistakes.

Then came the 'cat's whiskers' wireless, which we thought was wonderful. That was followed by the wireless set with the accumulator. Very often, when there was something interesting on, the accumulator would run out – and that was that! Then came the battery wireless sets (radios) and then television and now satellite television from all over the world. What a change!

When I was about nine years old, William Currington (known as 'Bib') said to me, "Are you coming with me down the marsh to fetch the cows up for milking?" The marsh was past the blacksmith's and Bib went every day to fetch the cows, with the big, old sheep-dog named Bob. The sheep-dog was 'bob-tailed', which was why he was called Bob. He was like a jolly great bear. I didn't know until afterwards that the old dog used to fetch the cows from the farthest field on his own. Old Bib was full of devilment, so he said to me, "You go and fetch the cows with the old dog and I will wait here for you. I shall tie a piece of cord on his collar and on your jacket, or he won't come with you." Bib tied the cord on my jacket - he knew what would happen, but I did not! When that was done, Bib said to me, "Are you ready?" and I said, "Yes." Then he said, "Go on, Bob," and the old dog pulled me over and dragged me along, face downwards, through all the mud and water, where the cows came through every day. It was up to our knees in mud, and Bob dragged me along until my coat tore and the dog broke away.

During my school days, Mr Farr used to thresh the stacks in what was called 'Dry Close.' (Now it is all new houses.) I spent every spare minute I could get there, killing rats and mice, of which there were thousands of all sizes. Many a time I have had mice crawling about inside my shirt and several times rats. The men all wore leg straps just below the knee, so that was as far as the mice could get.

I also went with my father, ferreting stacks and buildings for rats. My father always kept eight white ferrets for ratting, as polecats could easily be mistaken for rats and get shot. He had six polecats or whites for rabbiting, which he always kept separately.

When the stacks were being thrashed and they got to the bottom of the stack, we could see below where the rats went under the stack. My father went down on his knees, turned the stack bottom back and followed the runs which were full of rats of all sizes. He pulled the rats out by their tails and hit them with his boot to kill them. I soon got the idea, and joined him. It was a regular thing to get 300 or 400 rats out of one stack, especially at High Hayden. Mr Farr also farmed Cotton Farm and there were usually a lot of rats down there too.

After the threshing-tackle had been on a farm to thresh some corn stacks, there would be hundreds of small birds feeding on the rubbish where the drum had been standing. When the threshing engines or the steam ploughing engines were going from one farm to another, the farmer from where the the engines were leaving had to send a man to walk in front of the engines with a white flag. He was called the flagman.

Jordan and Addington and also Paine and Co, both of St Neots, used to come to collect corn from the farms with Foden engines with the body attached to carry the corn. I think their speed limit was five miles an hour. The engine driver of Jordan and Addington was Bill Smith of Eaton Socon and his mate was John Gentle of St Neots; Paine and Co's driver was Fred Bull of Eynesbury, but I am not sure of his mate's name. Us boys very much liked to see them.

The first car we saw in Yelling belonged to Dr Harrison from St Neots. It was a little, blue Austin and, when we were working in the fields at Yelling, we heard him leaving St Neots and coming up Paxton Hill. The car buzzed, just like a bumble bee.

The first plane I saw was in 1910, when us lads were playing Graveley lads at cricket at the back of Graveley Rectory. It was in the evening that we saw the plane which afterwards landed on Port Holme. It was piloted by Alan Moorhouse.

On Saturday June 10th, 1910, Yelling Cricket Team went to play Papworth Everard at Papworth on Mr Hooley's lovely cricket ground. I ran over to Papworth to watch the match, and although I was only nine years old at the time, I can clearly remember all that happened. Yelling batted and scored 186, then knocked Papworth out for 22, with my brother Charlie taking nearly all the wickets. My Uncle Jess, who usually batted at number three, was late arriving, so he batted at number five – and scored 61 not out. When Papworth batted, Harry Ding was clean bowled for a duck by Charlie, and, when he came back to the pavilion, he said, "Old Charlie is a good bowler. I never did like his bowling, and I never shall!" It seems just like yesterday.

These were the scores:

Yelling		**Papworth**	
James Meeks	29	H. Ding	0
W. Currington	28	A. Bennett	2
Billy Reed	13	H. Gates	1
E. Currington	0	E. Sibley	0
Jess Meeks not out	61	J. Ding	4
Joe Reed	1	B. Canwell	6
S. Currington	24	F. Sibley	0
T. Bruce	7	B. Desborough	0
W. Currington	7	F. Bennett	2
C. Meeks	4	B. Rolls	4
H Baxter	4	T. Sewell	1
Extras	8	*Extras*	2
Total:	**186**	**Total:**	**22**

When I was about nine years old, my job every Saturday was to clean knives, forks and spoons with a yellow powder called Bath-Brick. I had a board about two feet six inches long and six inches wide, with a strip of leather fastened to it. I would tip some Bath-brick on to this board and have a saucer of water beside it. I had a piece of rag, which I dipped in the water, then into the powder and rubbed it on the spoons. I had a bit of dry cloth to polish them, then that was the spoons done. Then I did the knives. I put some more Bath-Brick on to the board and a few spots of water and then rubbed the knives on the board until they were clean. Then, with the dry cloth, I would polish them until they were shiny. Last of all I did the forks. I hated that job!

My next job was cleaning shoes ready for Sunday. I used blacking for cleaning the shoes – the old kind, which was in blocks about one and a half inches square, wrapped in paper. I would take a square out of the paper and put it in a saucer or a tin lid, and mix it with a little water into a paste. I had a small brush to put the paste on to the shoes. Then I used another brush and had to keep on brushing until I got a shine on the shoes – this was a worse job than knife cleaning! Later on a new kind of polish came out, called 'Nugget', a paste in tins, which was a big improvement on the old blacking.

Another of my jobs was to fetch the kindling out of the wash-house into the house, ready for the morning. One evening, I was lighting a candle, ready to go into the wash-house, using *Wait-a-Minute* matches. When those matches were struck, they sizzled for about half a minute or so before they would light. As I struck one, the head flew off on to my celluloid collar and up it went in flames! It burnt my neck badly and my mother, trying to pull my collar off, burned her hands as well. My brother Buller was there too, wearing a corduroy jacket, and, when he threw his arms around my neck to put out the flames, he rubbed the flesh off my neck. Next morning, Dr White from Caxton came to see me and asked my mother what she had put on my burns. She told him she got the whitening pot that she used for whitening the hearth and had put that on. He said that was the best thing she could have done, but I was at home, off school, for ten weeks before my neck healed up.

Anthrax broke out on Mr Thomas Cubley Ashcroft's farm at Yelling in 1910 and all the cattle had to be burnt. I was at home from school, so I was able to sit at the window and watch three or four policemen building a huge wood fire in the little five-acre field near Yelling Chapel. (The site is now covered with houses, and the place where the fire was is where Mr Frank Reed lives.) The police were there for days and nights burning the cattle. They were there all the time and had a big waterproof sheet for shelter.

Mr Cubley Ashcroft used to ride about in a big, old four-wheeled carriage, drawn by an old horse which was very steady. The carriage was very low and had seats front and back. Old Mr Ashcroft would lay back in the back seat, looking very contented, and the old horse looked about the same! Most of the farmers rode around the fields on horseback. (Now they ride in pick-ups, Land Rovers and Range Rovers!)

When the Hounds were meeting at Kisby's Hut, Papworth Everard, or The Spread Eagle, Croxton, I would play truant from school and go to the meet. I would run with the hounds all day, finish up at Eltisley Wood and then run back to Yelling. I enjoyed it so much and could run all day and never get out of breath. It was a lovely sight to see the hounds in full cry; but when I got home, I would get a good hiding for playing truant – and another the next morning when I got to school!

In 1912, one lunchtime about one o'clock, when I was home from school for my dinner, I heard fox hounds in full cry coming down Mr Ashcroft's field, they came through the hedge close to our house and then on across Dry Close. Most of the horses went down the road and through the gate opposite the chapel, but Mr Jim Wakefield's horse jumped the high hedge, going partly over it and partly through it. I ran with the hounds across Dry Close, over the Yelling to High Hayden roadway, into Debden, then into Mr Wood's Grove, over the Rabbit Hut and into Mr John Green's field. I got in front of the hounds, so I stopped behind the hedge down the six acres. One of the dogs came and stood beside me. then the fox came through the hedge, close to where the dog and I were standing. The dog grabbed the fox and pulled it down about five yards from where I was standing. In a few seconds the whole pack was there. The Huntsman came on his horse and jumped off, and pulling out his knife, he cut off the fox's head, tail and four feet. Mr John Green had the head, his son Ernest Green had the tail and four other people had a foot each. Then I followed the hounds all through the woods at Croxton and on to Eltisley Wood and it was almost dark. My uncle Jessie was there, so he and I ran right the way back to Yelling – not a bad run!

Thinking about running, I remember that my uncle Jessie was quite a good runner. He was working on the road, near the Winteringham Farm entrance with Mr Stocker from Buckden, who also went running. The foreman was also with them. On the Monday morning, when they got to work, Mr Stocker, who had been racing over the weekend, was telling the others about winning the race, and he said to my uncle Jessie, "I will race you for a hundred yards for your racing bicycle against my week's wage." My uncle said "Okay, that's on." So the foreman stepped out 100 yards and said "When you are ready, I will drop my handkerchief for you to start," which he did. They ran side by side for 90 yards, then my uncle Jessie got about two yards in front –

and so he won Mr Stocker's week's pay.

When I was at school, there was just one motor in Yelling and that was a three-wheeled motorbike, owned by our schoolmaster, Mr E. J. Quick. It had two wheels in front, with a basket in between, and one wheel at the back.

One day in October 1986, I was going down Caxton End, Eltisley, to shoot some pigeons, when I saw Mr Ray Topham's men cleaning out a pond with a J.C.B. digger, which had a large bucket in front. It was scooping out the mud and tipping it into a trailer, which was being drawn by another tractor, and it brought back a vivid memory of pond cleaning in the year 1911. It was a hot, dry summer and the pond at New Zealand, which was at the west end of Yelling, was dry, so people decided to clean it out. The pond was used by the people of New Zealand for their water for all domestic purposes, except drinking. So, one morning, all the men and women from the eight cottages of New Zealand came to the pond with their buckets and got cracking. My father stood in the pond, filling the buckets. Two more men were in the pond: one was putting down the buckets for my father to fill and handing the full ones to another man, who was standing near the steps where the people went down to dip the water. That man handed them to the men and women, who were carrying the mud away in the buckets along the road and into Mr Ashcroft's field opposite New Zealand cottages. It was a nasty, dirty job. When the buckets were very full, they were quite heavy. The outsides of the buckets were very dirty, so the men tied pieces of sacking or cloth around their legs to keep their trousers as clean as possible. The women had sacks, cut open and tied around them, for the same purpose. The women didn't wear slacks or jeans in those days, and there were no Wellingtons either. I thought, "Whatever would happen if ponds had to be cleaned out by that method today?" I have a feeling that the ponds would stay as they were.

In those days, lots of people got their water for drinking purposes out of ditches, ponds where cattle went to drink or drain pipes that came off fields, as there was no mains water. Another thing I don't see today is the school children trudging off to school with their food bags slung over their shoulders. There were no school meals in those days and no buses to take them to school. It used to be a long drag for children living where I am now. They had to walk to Yelling School, as did the children from High Hayden Farm, Papley Grove and Hill Farm. They often had to stay at home while their shoes were being repaired.

Often we would see the five chaps from Toseland who belonged to the St Neots Town Band. They use to cycle from Toseland to St Neots two or three times a week for band practice in their uniforms. Their names were Arthur Sewell, Aubrey Surkitt, Dick Jakins, Cecil Hedge and Sam Hedge. My wife and I often cycled down to St Neots to hear the band playing for dancing on lawns and other special occasions.

How the country has changed since I was a boy! During the Spring and Summer, the grass fields were covered with cowslips, buttercups, daisies, dandelions, bluebells and many other wild flowers. The hawthorn hedges were all loaded with may blossom, and the crab-apple blossoms in the hedgerows were a picture. Butterflies of all colours fluttered around and there were bumble bees' nests of dried grass on the roadside.

After school hours, the children and their mothers were in the fields, picking cowslips and dandelions for wine-making, and there would be folk walking about the fields, looking for mushrooms. At harvest time, the women would be around the hedgerows, picking blackberries – but now so many hedgerows have been demolished. Walking along the hedgerows and ditches on a sunny day, I often saw snakes, lying curled up on the ditch banks, fast asleep, and all kinds of birds, sitting on their nests, or the young ones, peeping out of the nests; but I hardly ever see a snake these days. When it stopped raining, there were hundreds of frogs of all sizes, hopping about, also toads. Years ago, folk liked to see toads in their gardens, keeping insects under control. There were frogs and frog spawn on nearly every pond, brook or ditch that held water – hundreds of little black specks which formed into tadpoles, which would float about on the water. In time they became frogs and, on summer evenings, we would hear them croaking all the time, making a dreadful din! We also used to see lots of ladybirds, especially when we were carting maple-peas from the fields. We saw thousands of them when the carts were emptied. Years ago, I saw many wild birds, but many of them are dying out now – chaffinch, bullfinch, goldfinch, green linnet, wagtail, little tree climber, white-throat, barn owl, lark and cuckoo – those are just a few. There were hundreds of them about when I was a boy.

Wild pheasant and partridge are also on the decline owing to the ripping out of hedges, and the ditch banks being cut short with flail-cutters. There is no cover for them to nest in. The hedgehog nests on the ditch banks are being smashed to pieces and are gradually being wiped out.

A hedge sparrow built a nest in our garden hedge, and it laid four eggs. A cuckoo came and laid one egg in the nest as well, and the hedge sparrow sat on the eggs and hatched them all off. As the young ones grew up, the young cuckoo pushed the four young hedge sparrows out of the nest. The old hedge sparrow fed the young cuckoo until it could fly. We watched it every day, then, when it came out of the nest, it came to our door every morning to be fed. It did so on Christmas morning and, as we were feeding it, the rain was pouring down. Then the rain turned to snow and we had quite a deep snowfall – and that was the last we saw of our cuckoo.

When I was at school, if there had been a strong wind overnight, my mother would wake me early in the morning and tell me about the wind. Then up I would jump, get dressed and get my bag and run down what was called White Pond Close, as there were a lot of big elm trees where Yelling cricket pavilion is now standing. After a strong wind, there was generally a lot of kindling under the trees but, if I didn't get there early, I was unlucky, because there were a lot more children on the same job.

When I was young, Monday was wash-day. Early Monday mornings, I would see all the wash-house chimneys smoking, getting the old coppers boiling. Any old rubbish the women could get hold of went into the copper fire. Perhaps it would be a good thing if it still happened today – then maybe there wouldn't be so much rubbish lying around on the roadsides. There are not many of the old coppers on the go today. Life is a bit kinder to women nowadays; you no longer see them wearing those old coarse aprons, on their hands and knees scrubbing the floors. Thankfully, using the Whitening Pot to whiten the hearth and black-leading and polishing the fire grates and stoves are chores of the past.

When I was at school, and for some years after, all the beans which were wanted for seed were threshed with a flail to avoid splitting them. We had to be careful when using the flail, because it was easy to give ourselves a very nasty clout on the head. The beans were threshed on the barn floor and they were then cleared up and put through the dressing machine, coming out clean and ready for drilling. They were put into sacks, which held nineteen stones, and which all had to be lifted by hand – not like today when there are machines to do all the lifting.

In 1911, one of my old playmates, Sid Kidman, of Papley Grove, used to come down to Yelling to play cricket or football with us lads most Saturdays. One particular Saturday afternoon, Sid was riding one of the horses on the binder, cutting wheat, when they went over a wasps' nest. The wasps stung the horses and they bolted, throwing my old mate into the binder knife, which cut off both his arms, just above the elbows. But he grew into a big, fine chap and a collection was made for him to buy an organ to grind, and a pony to pull it around for him. He had another chap with him to play the organ. When he was around this area, he stayed at the Two Brewers public house in Cambridge Street, St Neots, where Mrs Richardson, dear old soul, looked after him like a mother. She cut up his food on a plate as if she was cutting it up for a little child, and he ate it off the plate like a dog.

Jim Norman the coalman from Yelling, had a dog which was very fast and could catch a hare in a very short distance. It used to walk to St Neots Allotment every day with Mr Norman to fetch coal for the village. Then, when Mr Norman got home, and we were at home from school, Mr Norman's son Jimmy and I would take the dog up to the top of New Zealand gardens, into Mr Farr's field, where there were a lot of hares. We would send the dog on to the field and very soon there would be a hare jumping up, and away the dog would go and would soon catch it. Then one evening Jimmy and I had the dog in what we called 'the Old Jetty', beside Mr Norman's cart shed, when two policeman came to us and we were frightened. We thought that they had come about the hares, but they had not. They said someone's dog had been worrying Mr Ashcroft's sheep, so they gave the dog something to make it sick. It brought up some sheep's wool, so they said that it was the guilty dog and it would have to be put down. That really broke our hearts, as we both loved that old dog.

I used to take my father's dinner up to High Hayden when they were threshing the corn stacks there. The men were all sitting in a row along the ditch bank and I sat with them while they were having their dinner. Bob Surkitt was telling the other men something which he didn't want me to hear. As he was talking, he suddenly stopped and said, "But little pigs have sometimes got big ears." Even though I was not very old, I got that all right!

In those days, the men in the village belonged to a Pig Club and every year they had a Pig Club Supper and everyone had either to sing a song or recite. I remember some of the songs they used to sing. My father's song was:

> *Oh, I feel just as happy as a big sunflower*
> *That nods and bends in the breeze,*
> *And my heart is as light as the wind*
> *That blows the leaves from the trees.*

Herbert Hills would sing:

> *Where did you get that hat, old boy?*
> *Where did you get that tile?*
> *Isn't it a nobby one -*
> *It's just the latest style!*
> *Oh, I would like to have one*
> *Just the same as that,*
> *Then wherever I would go, they'd say,*
> *"Where did you get that hat?"*

Then there was old Jim Todd – he was a scream. He would sing:

> *Slab, dab, slab, dab,*
> *Up and down the brickwork,*
> *Slab, dab all day long.*
> *In and out the corner,*
> *Round the Johnny Horner,*
> *Oh, what a rare old fancy corner,*
> *Slab, dab with the whitewash brush.*
> *Talk about a fancy ball,*

I put more whitewash on the old woman
Than I did on the garden wall.

He did all the actions while he was singing. One night they were so enthusiastic that he inadvertently punched a hole through the ceiling of the taproom!

In my younger days, when we were drilling the corn, we had four big horses on the drill, which was about six feet wide. There was a boy to lead the front two horses and another boy, a bit older, walked beside the horses with a whip to keep the horses going, and to see that each horse was pulling its share of the work. There was also a man holding the steerage on the drill in order to put the corn in as straight as he possibly could. The men steering the drills were more or less competing against each other. I often heard different folk saying that so and so's drilling had been the straightest they'd ever seen. That made every man who was steering the drill keen to do his very best. There was another man walking behind the drill and his job was to shut the corn off at each end of the field and wind the coulters up. If it was wet and dirty, the man carried a long 'spud' to keep the coulters clean, otherwise corn would lay on the top of the ground, to be eaten by the birds – rooks, pigeons, etc. Now, in all, there were four people involved, two lads and two men, with four horses and a six-foot drill. Nowadays, one man can do the job with one tractor and a drill 20 feet wide, and more. What a difference! When the horses were used, eight acres per day was a good day's work. When drilling, the horses had to be back in the stable by three o'clock; when ploughing, they were back by two o'clock. But with tractors, they can keep going indefinitely and drill many times that amount of acres.

Writing about ploughing has reminded me the the first Monday after the 6th January was what we called 'Plough Monday.' We used to pull a plough around the villages and sing songs – such as the one that went like this: "Please will you give the poor old ploughboy a ha'penny or a penny, or a bit of bread and cheese is better than nothing. Hail or rain, snow or blow, a-ploughing we must go. Remember us, poor ploughboys, a-ploughing in the snow."

Another song went like this:

> *Early in the morning, the ploughboy he is seen*
> *All hastening to the stable, his horses for to clean.*
> *With corn and chaff, he gives them a bait*
> *And combs their tails and manes out straight*
> *Again, ploughboy.*

I remember one team of ploughboys over 70 years ago. They took their plough out on Plough Monday evening to a certain farm. They sang their songs but nobody opened the door to give them anything – so they ploughed up the lawn! Luckily, I didn't happen to be in that team.

Ploughing today is very different to what it was when I was a boy. There were no tractors then, so all the land was ploughed by horses. It was a very slow job and we were ploughing from just after harvest, right through the winter and spring – that made quite a lot of spring drilling, which I do not see today. In my younger days, we had three huge horses to pull one plough, taking about a nine-inch furrow. On heavy land, there was a man and a boy with each plough. If we ploughed three roods by one-thirty in the afternoon, that was a good day's work. But on light land or sandy soil, we had two horses, side by side. One horse in the furrow and one horse on the land. That was much quicker and we could plough one acre per day with just one man. When working with three horses, the boy driving the horses carried a whip. He had a line from the hind horse's head, through a ring in the middle horse's halter and on to the halter of the front horse. If we were going to turn right (or turn off, as we used to say), the boy would jerk his line and say, "Gee-oh back, gee-oh back," and the horse knew just what he meant. If we wanted to turn left, the boy would pull his line and say, "Come hither, come hither," and the horse would turn left.

One morning, Mr Cullip, the horse keeper, and I were going to plough in the seed-field behind the New Zealand Cottages. It was a sharp, frosty morning and everywhere was all rime. Mr Cullip put a tin of grease on the aims ('aims' had hooks or chains to connect with the cart shafts) of the horse that I was riding. I was dreading hooking the horses on to the plough because the swelteries were covered with rime and it was so bitterly cold. I knew that was the job I had to do whilst Mr Cullip greased the plough wheels. I threw the tin of grease on the ground, noting where it fell, knowing he would send me back to find it.

That would keep me warm, and he would hook the horses on to the plough – before I got back! When we arrived in the field, Mr Cullip asked me for the tin of grease so he could grease the wheels of the plough, while I hooked the horses in. I said, "I haven't got it," so he said, "Well, you just go back and look for it" – which was just what I wanted him to say! I knew just where the tin was, and I was nice and warm, and, when I got back, the horses were all hooked to the ploughs! I often think about what I did then, even after all these years!

In 1911, Mr Cullip and I were cutting wheat with three horses on a binder in Mulberry Hayden, a field near High Hayden and the Old Gorse, on the Toseland to Croxton road. The first time round the field, we had two horses on the pole of the binder and one horse in the front, on the back of which I was riding. It was a young horse, so Mr George Baxter was leading it. We went over a wasps' nest, and the wasps stung the young horse, which almost got out of hand. No doubt it would have done if Mr Baxter had not been leading it. During the cutting of that field, we went over 13 wasp's nests. Mr Baxter dug one of them out and it was the size of a bushel measure. There were wasps' nests in almost every field in 1911 because it was a scorching hot summer.

When carting corn from the fields, one man from the farm, who was not in the harvest piece-work gang, would go and mow some green tares (common vetch) for the horses to eat while the carts were being emptied. At meal-times, we put some tares in the cart for the two horses that were in the field – one in the loaded cart and one in the empty cart. When we were carting at five o'clock in the morning, we had breakfast at eight o'clock and the men's wives or children rode out into the field in the 'breakfast cart' to bring a hot breakfast for the men. They came again at dinner-time, bringing a hot dinner and enough food for tea-time too. When carting, we had breakfast at eight o'clock, lunch at 11 o'clock, tea at four o'clock and a snack at six o'clock, then work on until dark. We then went home for our supper. Many a time, after we had eaten our supper, it was too hot to go to bed, so we went into the fields and slept on the stooks of corn.

When carting, the drivers had to take the horses down to the farm for them to have a drink at the horse-pond. One day, my brother Arthur took his horse to the pond, and, when he turned round to come out, the horse swung his head round (because of a gadfly) and the ring on the bit through its mouth got caught on a hook on the cart shaft. The horse ran back towards the back of the pond, where it was very deep. My brother jumped off into the water, leaving the cart under water – also the horse, which was covered apart from its head. No doubt the horse would have drowned but for Eben Corn, who walked into the pond, up to his neck, and unhooked the horse's head and led it out of the pond.

Most farmers also kept sheep, for which they grew mangolds, swedes and 'rabbies'. (A 'rabbie' was a kohlrabi, which is a kind of cabbage with a turnip-shaped stem.) When the plants were big enough to set out, the men would go ahead chopping out the distance the plants were to be left, but leaving two or three plants together. When the children came out of school, they went, with their mothers, to single out those plants, behind the men.

I went to Eltisley on two or three occasions to fetch hurdles from the hurdle-makers, Mr Fordham and his two sons, Ben and Ted. The hurdles were used for folding the sheep on the root crops. The farmer would also put the sheep on the wheat crops to bite it down; – it would then shoot out much thicker and there would be a big improvement in the crop.

I remember Mr Ray Topham and I and another man were loading some hay bales on to a trailer near High-Barns, when I noticed hundreds of crows in Mr Topham's winter barley. I said to Mr Topham, "Look at those crows in your barley." He said, "It looks as if they have got several acres of it down," and he told me to go down to the farm and ask his wife for his gun and a hundred cartridges, which I did. I arrived at the field as soon as I could, and, when I got there, I had never seen anything like it! I got into the bushes and shot those hundred cartridges in less than an hour, then I went to pick up the crows. Quite a lot of them were still alive and, as I picked them up, they made such a lot of noise. The other crows attacked me from all angles – they were simply mad! They nearly frightened the life out of me, but luckily I had taken my gun out with me, and it was a good job I did. I kept swinging the gun round: that kept the crows at bay, and killed three. While I was doing that, I walked backwards into the bushes to get out of danger. Then I got over the brook and walked along the other side, out of sight. The next morning, Mr Topham said,

"Harold, you had better take my gun and cartridges and have another go at those crows." So I went to the field – but there was not a single crow to be seen. It looked as if I had scared them, as well as them scaring me!

In the winter, the crop was folded off by the shepherd with stakes and hurdles. He made pens for the sheep, which allowed them to feed off the crop in sections. While one section was being fed off, the shepherd would be fixing another pen. It was a difficult job to drive the stakes in the ground when it was frozen. The shepherd had a hut on wheels, which could be moved about the field as he liked and in which he kept some other food for the sheep, such as 'locust beans', etc. Us kids used to put the 'locusts' in our pockets to eat ourselves!

Years ago, most children would have a pet bird – jackdaw, magpie, or a brown linnet or goldfinches in a cage. We had a pet jackdaw, which came and sat on our shoulders when we were having our meals. Quick as a flash, it would nip the spoon out of our saucers and, if the door was open, it would fly out and hide the spoon. Sometimes it took a fork or coins – anything that was shiny. The poor old bird was scared to death of thunder and lightning and, when a storm was raging, it hid in any handy nook or cranny.

When we were caging brown linnets, we took the cage to the nest and put the nest into the cage before the young ones were ready to fly. Each day, we moved them a few yards nearer the house until we got them home. Then we put them on the wall outside and, if we were lucky, the parent birds would still come and feed them. But sometimes we were unlucky, because, when we got them home, the old birds would give their young a poison weed and kill the lot. To get goldfinches, we bought some bird-lime and kept a lookout for where there were some big pod-thistles – that was where the goldfinches would come to feed. When we found out where they were feeding, we got some rushes and put bird-lime on them and lay them on the thistles. When the finches went on to the thistles, they got some lime on their wings and could not fly, so we took them home, cleaned their wings and put them into a cage. That was made illegal a long time ago.

At Graveley, they used to hold a flower show, and, around 1912, when I was still at school, there was an entry for 'A Bouquet of Wild

Flowers'. The show was open to three villages, Graveley, Toseland and Yelling, and a lot of children entered, including me. As I went about the fields a lot, more than most of the children, I got a much better selection of flowers than they did. When I took my flowers into the tent and folk saw that I had Asparagus, Canterbury Bells and Cornflowers, they said, "You want to take those out or you will be disqualified because they are not wild". A lot of people told me that, including Mrs Quick, the schoolmistress, but I said, "No, I will take a chance", and left them in the bouquet. The tent closed at 12 o'clock and, when it opened again at two o'clock, there was a ticket on mine – 1st Prize! Several people went to the judges and said, "Harold Meek's are not wild". But the judges said, "Yes, they are quite in order". So I won that year, and the next one too!

Another day we used to look forward to each year was the first Sunday after the 25th September – 'Yelling Feast'. As kids, we would stand on the road outside our houses, waiting for the Feast (fair) vans to arrive. There would be old Mrs Welch (a nice old girl), her son Bill and her daughter Fanny. They always had their stalls outside The White Swan and their living van backed into the Mash Gateway. (It was called 'Mash', which might have been 'Marsh' originally, as the ground beyond certainly was marshy and damp.) They would be open on Monday and Tuesday, then they would pack up on the Wednesday morning, which seemed sad to us kids.

One year, Bill Welch's Shooting Gallery was there and my uncle George was having a few shots when a big tramp came walking round. He was watching my uncle shooting and said "I will take you on – ten shots at the bull, and the loser pays". My uncle said "Okay, you are on" and they tossed a coin to see who would go first and my uncle won. He scored ten bulls. Then the roadster took his turn and he scored nine bulls, but missed the tenth one. My uncle said, " Well now you know what you have got to do, don't you? You have got to pay up". But the tramp said, "I'm not going to pay". So my uncle said,"You will either pay up be paid, just as you like" – so he paid up!

When we had our Harvest holidays from school, and I was about ten years old, I went 'leading shock horse', from one shock to another, for the men to cart the corn. But before carting, I was riding the horses on the binder (which cut the standing corn and tied it into sheaves, which were stooked or made into a shock) day after day, from morning to night. The hardest job was to stop falling asleep. The cutting horses would work from about 8 am to 11 am, then change again at 2 pm and again at 5 pm, three horses each time.

What a difference there is on the farms today from when I was a boy, when I would see gangs of men and women working in the fields. The men would be hoeing the corn, each man taking four rows of wheat or barley. I remember my father and five more men hoeing the wheat at Old Farm, Yelling. It was rather a rough job and the men kept grumbling and saying they couldn't do it for the price they were getting. As my father was the head of the gang, he went to see old Mr Farr, who was the governor, and told him that the men couldn't do the work for that price – but Mr Farr wouldn't listen. So my father followed him from one farm, to another and in the end Mr Farr said, "Well, Walter, I shall give you another penny an acre – and that is all I can afford".

The women would be picking thistles or pulling out docks, charlock or wild parsnip. I would sometimes help sowing clover seed in the corn about June time, I used what was called a 'seed barrow', which had two handles, one wheel and a box about eight yards long full of clover seed. A man held the handles and I had a rope to pull the barrow along, which got a bit tiring by the end of the day!

If it was too wet for harvest work, us boys would be tying string for thatching. This was the string which had been saved from the sheaves when they were being threshed. At times, it became a bit boring, sitting there in the barn from seven o'clock in the morning to seven o'clock at night. When the weather was dry and we were working in the fields, we had one great big mare, called 'Diamond'; when she had been away for her foal for a time, the milk would run from her. I had gallons of it to drink and often filled my drink bottle up with it.

In 1912, the Titanic went down, and I think St Neots Paper Mill was burnt down in the same year. I remember a song children used to sing about the sinking of the Titanic. It went like this:

   'Be British,' was the cry as the ship went down.

Every man was standing at his post.
Captain and crew, when they knew the worst,
Saving the women and the children first.
'Be British,' was the cry, the fate which proved unkind,
Would those, who are willing
Give a penny or a shilling
To those who are left behind?

When I was at school, people in the village of Yelling used to bring their cutting tools, trimming hooks, axes, bills, shears, clippers, knives, scissors and razors for my father to sharpen. He got so many that he said, "I must build a machine to do all this grinding" – which he did. He built it in the barn and us boys had to sit and pedal it for him. But we often wanted to play cricket in the evenings, so my father altered it a bit so he could pedal it himself. He also did the hair-cutting and shaving for lots of people, not only in Yelling but in other villages as well.

When I was a boy at school, there was an old man whose name was John Tack (often known as Jack), and his daughter Clare, who lived in a small mud and plaster cottage, close to the road opposite Friends Farm, Yelling. John was blind, but they had a little shop where they sold a few sweets and things like matches, candles etc. The tea was in lead packets. When our mothers asked us lads to go to Mr Tack's to buy a quarter of tea, we would take the tea home and our mother tipped it into the tea-tin and gave us back the packet. We ran back to Mr Tack's shop with the packet rolled up into a ball. As it was pure lead, we received a halfpenny a packet. Then we would go down the village to Mr Wood's shop at the end of Garland Row and buy two sticks of rock, which were about nine or ten inches in length. They had transfers wrapped around them, which we wetted and stuck on the backs of our hands. We thought it looked as if we had been tattooed, and all for a halfpenny.

One Sunday, coming home from Church Sunday School, Jim Norman, my brother Stan and I met poor old John Tack, up near Mont Shepherd's house. Because John was blind, he had a big stick. Jim Norman, who was walking in front of my brother and me, grabbed hold of the stick as he passed by John, who swung his stick at Jim Norman, but caught both my brother and me on the back of the head, as we were walking hand in hand – and we hadn't done anything!

As boys, most Saturdays, Jim Norman and I used the old sack barrow to take chaffs, oats and straw from the mill barns down to Jim's father's stable. If old Yelling Mill was working, we would go up the steps into the mill with Reynold (Ren) Hayden, who was doing the grinding. If he got the chance, Ren would roll us in the meal that he was grinding – then we got a row when we returned home for being in such a mess.

All through the summer, Jack Dudley of Offord, who had his own horse and cart, used to cart great big granite stones. He used to tip a cart-load about every hundred yards, ready for the roadman to put on the roads with his barrow and shovel. The roadman put a layer about 18 inches wide along each cart track and he would leave about 18 inches or two feet along the middle of the road, where I had to cycle. If there was a low place in the middle, he would put a layer of stones there. When I rode over them, I often got a burst tyre.

I first learned to ride a bike when I was at school. My brother bought the old bike, which had solid tyres, from Tom Catmull of Toseland for three shillings. It had no mudguards and the tyres were in pieces, tied in with string and wire. I learned to ride in the fields and, the first time I rode it, I didn't know how to get off – and it had no brakes! So I ran it into the ditch and fell off. That was the only way I could think of.

Thinking about shaving, I remember George Sawford, the barber at St Neots Market Square. He was a real comedian! One evening, a man from Eaton Socon went into his shop for a shave. When Mr Sawford had lathered his face, ready for shaving, he took his cut-throat razor and held it in front of the man's face and whispered, "Did anyone see you come in here?" The man said, "No." "Well," said Mr Sawford, "I will take good care that no-one will see you go out." And the man jumped out of the chair, with his face covered in lather, and ran across the Market Square as fast as he could run. That amused Mr Sawford very much!

When I was at school, and Yelling were playing cricket at home, in John Green's field, if the weather was nice, Alf Sibley (who kept The White Swan public house in Yelling) would bring the teas into the cricket field: a barrel of beer, crates of minerals and sweets, etc. Those were lovely times. If Yelling were playing at High Papworth (Papworth Everard), or at Low Papworth (Papworth St Agnes), Graveley, Croxton or Eltisley, as soon as I was out of school, I would run to either place as fast as my legs would carry me to watch the cricket. If Eltisley were playing at home, I would also run there – to see George Rose bat. I loved to see him bat for his big hitting. I always said he stood alone as a big hitter, and Claud Lovitt of St Neots stood alone as a stylish batsman. I have played with, and against, both men many a time.

When my mother wanted me to run errands for her, I always had my iron hoop, as I could go much quicker with that. One day, Walter Cullip got my hoop and rolled it against old Jack Tack's legs who grabbed hold of it and kept it for a very long time. He wouldn't let me have it because, being blind, he thought I had rolled it against him on purpose.

One Sunday morning, several young chaps from Yelling were playing pitch-ha'penny near the Top Planting (plantation). An old tramp, wearing a ragged cap and coat, came and sat on a stone heap for a while, then walked along and stood with them for a few minutes, watching them play. Then one of the chaps noticed something which told him the 'tramp' was a 'copper', so he grabbed the money and started to run. It *was* a policeman, and he blew his whistle and up came another one! Six of the chaps had to go to Caxton (Court) and were each fined half a crown (two shillings and sixpence = 12 1/2p).

When I was a boy, London school children used to come to Yelling for a holiday. One afternoon, when my mother was in the wash-house, she was standing near the window, facing Dry Close, where there were several straw stacks. She saw two of the London boys against one of the stacks and then she saw it burst into flames. The boys ran away. I had been to market in Ben Reed's four-wheeler, and was returning along Toseland Road when we met my brother Arthur on Lady Robert's old crippled nag, going to get the fire engine. He shouted as he went past, "Dry Close is on fire!" Arthur went to the fire station, but they could not get any horses for a long time. In the end, they got two from Andy Baxter and arrived at the fire at five o'clock. Then it took one hour to get steam up before they could start work. The fire had been going for about four hours!

In 1911, when my father was thatching in Dry Close, with William Currington (known as 'Otty') serving him, he asked me to fetch two bottles of Oatmeal Stout from The White Swan. As I was walking along Granny Beck's close, I was singing, with a bottle in each hand, swinging to and fro. They banged together and smashed. I went and told my father what had happened and he just said, "Well, you had better go and fetch two more." Poor old Otty was killed in the First World War.

Each year, when it was Yelling Chapel Anniversary, we used to have tea in Mr Ashcroft's barn. There was a big white sheet with red letters which said, 'Welcome'. After tea, we used to have sports in Granny Beck's Close, which we very much enjoyed.

Summer 1911 was very hot – it was a real scorcher; but 1912 was a soaker! My father had been to St Neots Market, when the floods came. He said people were coming down the High Street in boats. In 1912, harvest was the wettest I have ever known. The rain poured down for a whole week and absolutely no harvest work was done. The sheaves of corn which had been cut were laying in several inches of water. When the weather cleared and we started work again, we were picking sheaves up and standing them in water. There were no Wellingtons at that time, so we tied pieces of cloth and anything we could get hold of over the lace-holes of our boots to keep the water out. I remember hearing folk say that half the corn at the south of St Neots came down the river into the lock-gates at the paper mill. When I went to St Ives with Mr Cullip to take the portable engine to Rustons to be overhauled, as we were going along the Hilton road, Mr Cullip said to me, "Look, boy, at those sheaves up in the bushes, along that brook." The sheaves had floated down the brook. When we carted the wheat from the fields to the stack, the water was running out of the bottom of the carts, and the man in the field, who was pitching the sheaves on to the cart, had to wear a raincoat, because the water was running out of the sheaves all over him, as he lifted them above his head. We had two horses on each cart to get the corn out of the fields, and, when we got to the gateway out of the field, we had to keep the cartwheels running in the same tracks. The ruts were so deep that the axle was scraping the ground. When the wheat was threshed out of the stacks just before the next harvest, the sheaves were as hard as boards

– but the wheat was lovely and bright. That year, the 'draggins' and seed clover were left in the fields.

When I was a boy, most householders kept a pig in a sty and, when the pigs were fat enough for killing, people would come and ask my father if he would come and kill the pigs for them, not only in Yelling, but in other villages as well. When he went to cut them up, the people would all give him a nice joint of pork, so we always had plenty in salt, kept in a big stone pot. This was about three feet six inches highs so it held quite a large amount. When my father killed the pigs at home, I would take the large enamel bowl up to him, to catch the blood, then take it down to the house, where my mother would make Black Puddings. She also made sausages. There was homemade lard, fritters, pig's fry and chitterlings. My father kept the bladder of each pig and he had a list of names, because the men in the village liked pigs' bladders for tobacco pouches. He blew each bladder up with a bicycle pump and hung it up to dry. When it was well dry, it was ready for another customer. There was no waste!

A man's wage on the farm at that time was two shillings and tuppence per day – 13 shillings a week (65p)! My father told me that Mr Achurch of Lower Wintringham asked if he would put some main drains in for him, so my father used to walk from Yelling to Lower Wintringham, dig three chains of main drain, three feet deep, pipe up and fill in – and then walk back to Yelling. All for two shillings and sixpence per day. That was tenpence a chain, which was 22 yards long!

My father was never short of reminiscences. He used to tell us children about a man from Yelling who was walking to St Neots along the Toseland Road when he met a plague of rats. They came towards him in the pitch dark, squealing, and the man ran back to Yelling, almost scared to death. He would also tell us about the bullock which was roasted on the ice on the river at St Neots. I think he said it was in the year 1900. That must have been a sharp winter!

My father and some other men were working in the Old Gorse Allotment and, while they were having dinner, Charlie Bundy, the gamekeeper's son, who was only five years old, came along. One of the men, Eben Corn, asked him if he would like a mince pie. Charlie said, "Yes, please," so he ate the mince pie and nothing was said.

When the men started work they said goodbye to Charlie. He said, "Good-bye" – but he also said to Mr Corn, "Tell your mum to put more meat in the pies tomorrow." That made the old men laugh.

My father talked about, and had a good laugh about a Yelling man named Henry Currington (nicknamed Nappy). He was a very big man who always nodding his head and blinking his eyes and stuttering. One day he was sitting in the doctor's surgery at Caxton, and Dr Giles, who was mixing the medicine, lit up a cigarette. So Henry pulled out his clay pipe and lit that. Dr Giles said, "If you don't put your pipe out, I shall put you out." And Henry, nodding his head, blinking and stuttering said to Dr Giles, "You can start on that job as soon as you like." My father often laughed about that. Henry went to live in London, but he often came down to Yelling to help with the harvest.

Once, up at High Hayden Farm, when the ferrets were in a stack, we saw the thatch lifting. My father got a ladder and opened the thatch, to find that the ferret had got a wood-pigeon, which was sitting on the nest with two eggs. My father and I often went around the stacks at night with a light and a stick, to knock the rats off the side of the stacks – what my father didn't kill, the dogs did.

On another occasion, Alec Surkitt, living at High Hayden, mixed a heap of food for his bullocks, ready for feeding next morning. He went back into the barn during the evening with a lantern and found the food covered with rats, which had partly cleared it up. They ran everywhere, squealing and frightened Mr Surkitt almost to death!

Mr Surkitt went straight down to Yelling to see Mr Farr, by whom he was employed, and told him that he would never go into that barn again unless something was done about the rats. Mr Farr came to see my father, told him what had happened, and asked him if he would go and set about them, which he did. The next day, my father threw a very small ferret on the barn roof, then he stood in the barn and shot 76 rats, without moving, as they ran along the beam. A lot went past him while he was reloading.

My father always loaded his own cartridges for ratting – with half a charge of powder and half of shot. As a boy, I liked to sit on the floor with a sheet of cardboard and a wad cutter cutting wads for my father. When they threshed the stacks at High Hayden, it was a regular thing to get 300 or 400 rats out of one stack.

During the harvest holidays from school, I walked behind the binder cutting the corn, carrying a stick, I watched for the ears of corn to move, then I knew a rabbit was hidden. I struck with my stick and it was very seldom that I missed. I very often got 50 or 60 rabbits in a day. When cutting seed clover, I would fill my pockets with pebble stones and kill a lot of rabbits that way. I would throw as straight as I could shoot. And, as a boy, I could tell the make of every bird's nest.

For several years, in my younger days, the Cambridgeshire Point to Point used to be run on Mr Wakefield's farm at Caxton. I remember John Woods of Church Farm, Yelling, running a horse called 'Hotspur' – and it could move too! It was at the front of Mr Bank's horse, when they came to the brook. Mr Bank's horse bumped it and knocked 'Hotspur' into the brook, but the jockey got it out, mounted it again and came fourth.

During my school days, us kids sat about in the grass fields and ate a lot of green leaves (we called them cock-sorrel); but you do not hear of it today. In my young days, people in the village made their own enjoyment. We had dancing in the school, and at Feast times in Alf Sibley's barn at The White Swan to the music of the melodian. Some villages had their own concert party. Yelling Concert Party would visit Abbotsley, then Abbotsley Concert Party would visit Yelling, which made for very enjoyable evenings. Whenever there was a circus at St Neots, Ben Reed took a load of people in his two-horse four-wheeler – another nice evening out.

In those days, all the men worked on the farms. There was no Sunday work, apart from feeding the horses and cattle. There was only one newspaper in the village, *The News of the World*, which came by post to David Howlett. There were no telephones.

A man used to lead a stallion around the villages from farm to farm. It looked very nice with its mane all braided up with brass and many coloured ribbons. (Something we do not see today.) The sight of mares and foals out in the grass fields is a thing of the past. We saw foals suckling and then kicking up their heels and jumping about.

When I was at school, Nathen Reed had a horse, which I took on to the roadside to graze for an hour before I went to school and another hour each evening after school for a penny an hour. That was tuppence each day for six days, which meant I was earning a shilling (5p) each week!

Before I was old enough to start work, when the harvest holidays came, we would watch for the first field of corn to be cleared after they had carted the corn out of the field. If they left one or two sheaves in the middle of the field, we knew we could not go gleaning, but, as soon as they took the sheaves away, we knew it was 'all clear'. Then the women and their children would flock into the field and lay their sheets, or bags cut open, on the ground. They put on their gleaning bags – tied round their waists, with bags hanging in front, in which to put the short ears of corn or ears with no stalk. The ears on long straw would be bunched into a rosette, tied round with a piece of straw, then the bunches were laid on the sheet on the ground. The short ears in the gleaning bags were tipped into sacks. We would tie up the sacks, so the ears didn't fall out. When the sheets with the bunches of corn were full, we would take two corners and tie them together also. Then we would lay down some more sheets. When we had finished, we carried the bags of ears and the sheets of bunches home and stored them in a dry place until harvest was finished and all the gleaning done.

We had to wait until they threshed the allotment holders' corn, which was stacked in small stacks in Mr Harry Stocker's yard. Each allotment holder had his own stack, so every man had to be there to help to thresh. When they had finsihed, the the gleanings were threshed, each person's corn kept separately. The barley gleanings were kept for poultry food and the wheat was taken to St Neots, to Mr Hinsby's mill, to be ground into flour. So most families had a sack of flour standing in the house. It came in very handy, as quite a number of people in those days baked all their own bread.

I remember going on a Sunday School outing to Skegness. We had just got to the sands, when one of the lads, Billy Peak, said, "I want to go to the toilet." We saw a toilet on the sands and he popped in. He had just sat down on the seat, when the man who the toilet belonged to rushed in and said to him, "You didn't pay to come in here." Billy said, "I didn't know I had to pay." The man said, "Oh yes, it is tuppence to use this toilet." Billy said, "Ah well, I'm not going to use it then," and he rushed out. Just outside the toilet, he did his business on the sands. Billy said, "I wasn't going to pay tuppence to do that, as I only have threepence for my whole day's outing."

At that time, if there was a death in the village, one church bell would be tolled very slowly for about an hour. Before a service, all the bells would be ringing up to five minutes before the service started, then only one bell would be rung. We could hear people hurrying by, saying, "That is the five minute bell, we shall have to hurry or we shall be late." We could also hear the bells ringing on Sunday mornings in other villages, which was a lovely sound. For a wedding, all the bells would be rung. There was a saying that Toseland was the only church where they rang all the bells for a funeral and only one for a wedding. The joke was that there was only one bell in Toseland church! When I was 11 years old, I was presented with a bible as a special prize for attending Sunday School at Yelling Church every Sunday throughout the year.

For several years I used to go to Dr White's at Caxton three days each week to fetch medicines for patients in the village. George or Tom Leach came with me, because, at times, we had a lot of bottles of medicine to carry. We were scared of meeting tramps from the Caxton Workhouse. One day, on our way home at about one o'clock, we had collected two or three baskets of medicine, so we stopped to have a rest and talk to Tom Baxter and his son Fred, who were working on the road near Crows Nest Farm. They were cutting the grass verges with a mattox (mattock), which Fred Baxter was holding at the time. Two tramps came along and they thought we had brought the roadmen's dinnner in the baskets. One of the tramps said, "Come on, we are going to have some of that," but the other one said, "No." Then the first tramp said, "Come one, let's have some," and came towards us. Fred Baxter held the mattox up and said, "If you come near here, mate, I'll part your bloody hair with this." The tramp changed his mind and they walked on.

Another time, a tramp came into Dr White's surgery to ask for some hot water. Dr White said, "I will give you a dose of poison that will boil your insides for you." But Dr White was a really good doctor and a firm believer in Epsom salts. He used to say that if they were a guinea (twenty one shillings) an ounce, there would be a great demand for them. But, as they only cost a penny an ounce, people were not interested in them, although they were the best thing you could have in the home.

In Toseland there was an old lady, Miss Andrews, who pushed a big heavy old truck with iron tyres to St Neots two or three times a week to fetch paraffin, crocks and all sorts of things, which she took round the village to sell. One day, she came down the Church Hill in Yelling and the truck became master of her. She couldn't keep up with it, so she let go of the handles and the truck turned over. The paraffin, crocks and all the lot were strewn all over the road. Poor old gal!

In 1912, I was going home from school with several other children. At Yelling Cross, near Cross Pond, at the entrance to the Manor Farm, we saw Mr Linford the builder from St Neots, who had his men working there. They were putting a drain in from Yelling Cross down to the brook near The White Swan public house. The concrete and iron gratings are still there on the left, going down what we called Mont Shepherd's Hill. Mr Linford said, "Come here, you children. Do you want to earn some pocket money?" We said, "Yes." So he said, "Here is sixpence for anyone who can spell scissors." I said, "I can," and I spelled it correctly. Then he asked us to spell "physics" and then "competition" – I spelled both words and got another two sixpences. Now one shilling and sixpence was a lot of money in those days. Mr Linford said, "That is all for today, but I will see you again tomorrow with some more words for you to spell – but they will be harder and I will give you a shilling for each correct answer!" I went home and laid the three sixpences on the table. My mother said, "Wherever did you get all that money from?" I told her, and also that I would have some more money the next day – and I said it might be even more! Next day, there was Mr Linford waiting for us. "Now, there will be a shilling if you can spell Nebuchadnezzer," he said. I said, "I can," and spelled it correctly and got my shilling. The next word was "diarrhoea," which I spelled correctly and got another shilling. "Well," he said, "that's the lot. I sha'n't see you again, as we finish work here today." I took the two shillings home to my mother. It came in very handy as money was very scarce in those days. I had earned three shillings and sixpence very easily, I thought. When I started work, I only got three shillings for a week's hard work!

In those days, there were three donkeys in Yelling village. Milly Fields had one, Joe Reed had one and so did Mark Shepherd. When they were pulling their carts, Billy Field's and Mark Shepherd's donkeys would not go as fast as you could crawl, but Joe Reed's donkey ran as fast as any pony or a good many nags. I have been with my mother and Joe Reed's wife to St Neots station to fetch people off the train, and it did not take long, because the old donkey went flat out all the way there and all the way back and never eased up. I always looked out for Joe Reed (keeper of Yelling Post Office), when he came by our house to take letters to Graveley Post Office, since he would take us for a ride as he delivered the letters.

Later on in my school days, the children from Croxton, Eltisley, Yelling and Toseland were invited by Sir Douglas and Lady Newton to a tea party in the park each year. The tables were laid outside on the grass opposite the estate office. The Yelling and Toseland children were taken to Croxton in Mr Farr's wagon, with one horse on the wagon driven by the horse keeper, Mr Cullip. When tea was finished, the sports were held in front of the house between the house and the lake. The Yelling and Toseland children raced against the Croxton and Eltisley children. The ship which I won in a race in 1912 was proudly displayed on the wall in our house for years. During the time we were in the park, most of us were taken for a ride around the lake in the motorboat, which was very much enjoyed.

Also during my school days, there was a farm sale at John Green's farm at the top end of the village. I knew that Mr Green had some mole traps which I wanted, so, when I came out of school at 12 o'clock, I ran up to the farm as fast as I could. I went straight to the mole traps and stood there until they were sold. There were 27 traps and I bought them for three shillings. (I am still using them after 79 years.) I hadn't had the traps long when I caught 13 moles in one trap during one morning, and they have caught hundreds since. During The Great War, mole skins were worth two shillings and threepence each.

To save their crops, the farmers in my school days would pay us boys a penny for six young sparrows, a penny for three old sparrows and a penny for a dozen sparrow eggs.

One night, Mr Norman the gamekeeper, who lived in the Keeper's House up in the Old Gorse Allotments, was troubled by poachers in the New Gorse. His son, Harry, was out, so he went after the poachers alone. The poachers got hold of him, pushed his head down in a great big hole and drove a stake tightly down between his legs, so he could not move. When his son came home and his father was not there, he went to look for him. And that was how he found him.

There were two allotments in Toseland, one on the Toseland Cross, which has now gone in with Mr Warboy's farm, and the other was called the Old Gorse Allotment, which has now gone in with Mr Ray Topham's farm. At Yelling, there was the Mill Allotment, opposite the old windmill, which was taken down in 1915 because of the Yelling Airfield. In the Mill Yard, which is now owned by Mr Frank Reed, stands a small barn, which, during the First World War, was used a a bomb dump and was surrounded by sandbags. That allotment is owned by Mr Gordon Ashcroft. The second Yelling allotment was the Wood-Field Allotment, which is now owned by Mr Charles and Jim Sells. The third allotment was the Bottom Plantation Allotment, which now goes with Mr Roger Pinner's farm. So all the allotments have gone – nobody wants allotment work today.

Over eighty years ago, a tree on the Toseland Cross Allotment was struck by lightning during a very heavy storm, and an ash tree at the back of Mr Wood's farm at Yelling was also struck at the same time. I remember the storm very well, it was on a Saturday morning and I had just been down to the village to old Mrs Wood's shop to get our groceries. Her shop was at the end of Garland Row and I had just given her my order. I then walked along the road as far as the group of cottages near The White Swan and stopped to have a word with old Joe Catmull, who was standing in his garden. While I was speaking to him, there was a rumble of thunder. Joe said, "It's thundering nice," and, at that second, there was a sharp flash of lightning and a crash of thunder – and the rain just poured down. I ran back to Mrs Wood's shop and stayed with her until the storm was over: it was certainly a nasty one. Edith Howlett, a school teacher, who lived next door to us, was in Huntingdon at the time and didn't know that there had been a storm. She hadn't even heard the thunder. They say you can only hear thunder for seven miles – so that appears to be about right!

On Saturdays, during my school days, I went up to Mr Woods at Church Farm, Yelling, to do jobs – cleaning mangolds and grinding them for the cattle and horses. While I was grinding them into a scuttle under the grinder, I used to pick up a nice slice and eat it, which was very tasty if it was a nice Yellow Globe and had been in the pit for quite a while. For my Saturday work, Mr Woods paid me sixpence. One day, Old Billy Fields, the harness maker, came into the yard and the old boar saw him and ran straight at him. The boar ripped his leg open from his knee to his hip with its tusks and made a terrible mess of the leg.

One Saturday, I went to the farm across the fields for a short cut. When I got to the bottom of Dove House Close, at the back of Yelling School, I came over the brook at the bottom of the close, where there is a very steep hill. There I saw Mr David Howlett and his son and David Woods with three horses and chains. They were going to move an enormous tree trunk, which they had cut down the day before – it really was a large one. It lay at the top of the steep hill and they wanted to get it down on to the level ground, so they could fix it to a gib to cart it away. They rolled the long chains round it and hooked the horses on the chains to roll it along. While they were hooking the horses on, I moved from where I had been standing, watching, and it was a good job I did! When they went to move the tree, the chains broke and the tree came down the hill and into the brook at the bottom at a terrific pace, just where I had been standing! It is still there to this day.

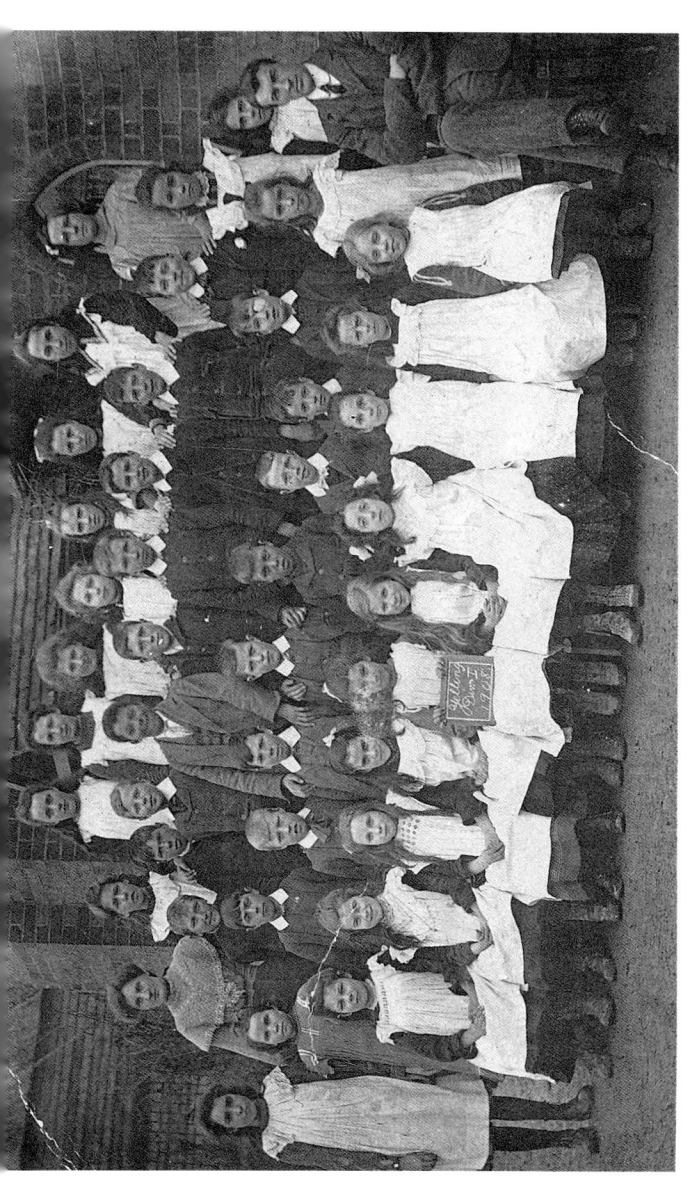

Yelling School, Division 1 – 1908

Back row Beatrice Topham (*third from left*)

Third row Teacher standing is Winifred Woods; the third boy along (discounting the girl om a row by herself) is Harry Lunnis and the last boy is Arthur Meeks

Second row Walter Meeks (5th *from left*), 6. George Howlett, 8. Walter Reed (Walt), 9. William Peak, 12. Headmaster, Mr E.J. Quick

Front row 1. Beatrice Stocker, 6. Margaret Brown (married brother Arthur), 10. Elsie Franklin

This photograph shows local men, all in the Duke of Bedford's Regiment. It was taken on Easter Monday 1916 at the front of Miss Hedge's shop in Yelling.
Back row Percy Norman, Joseph Currington (Joe), Ernest Revell, William Currington (Otty) killed in 1916, Thomas Hedge (Tom) killed in 1916, Thomas Reed (Tom), Walter Currington (Phip)
Front row William Currington (Bib), Ernest Currington killed in 1916, Albert Currington killed in 1916

Yelling Mill – 1900

This photograph, belonging to Frank Reed shows the mill which stood on the right hand side of the Toseland to Yelling road, half-way between the Toseland crossroads and the New Zealand cottages. It was used for grinding flour by Ronald Hadyn who worked for Thomas Ashcroft. The mill was taken down in 1915 to make way for the Yelling Airfield. The men standing on the mill are Mr Norman and Mr Woods.

Mary-Ann Wheal and Robert Wheal (Bobby) of Barns Farm. They had four daughters, Mary, Emma, Rose and Elizabeth. One Saturday evening in 1910, a balloon from France, carrying 3 Frenchmen, landed in the Old Gorse allotment. Mr Bobby Wheal came with his horse and cart and took the balloon and its crew down to St Neots station.

Croxton Saw Mill in the 1920s

Goog Thody is the boy holding the horse

2. Hard Working Days

When I left school and started to work for Mr Farr of Manor Farm, Yelling, in 1914, one of my first jobs was to go with Sid Currington to one of the Croxton plantations, which was called 'The Boards.' We went to get a load of privet for making bands to go round bunches of wood, which were called faggots. Every few years, Mr Farr would leave a nice whitethorn hedge to grow up to about nine or ten feet high. He kept it trimmed both sides so that it was nice and narrow; then, when the wood in the hedge was about the right thickness, he would send the men to cut it down. It had to be laid out nice and straight so that it was better for handling. When it was all cut down, the men would have a chopping block each and a bill-hook and they also wore leather gloves, as the whitethorn had got quite a lot of thorns on it. Then they would get spaced out down the hedge and would use the privet we had fetched from Croxton to make bands ready to go round the faggots. To make a band, they would put one end on the ground, place one foot on it, then twist the other end, making a loop under the foot, then lay it on the ground. They chopped the wood into lengths of about three feet and laid it on the band until they had enough for a faggot. Then they put the end which had been twisted through the loop at the other end, put their foot on the faggot, pulling the band tight, then the end was put under the band, so it wouldn't come loose – and that was one faggot. Then they did the same – again and again. For all that the men got was tuppence per faggot. As they made them, they put them in small heaps ready to be carted away, which Sid Currington and I used to do with a horse and cart. We took them to the farm and built a stack in the orchard, quite close to the farmhouse. Then the faggots could be fetched in when needed to be used in the wash-house, or on the open hearth, where there were two or three large hooks hanging over the old fireplace, with great big pots on them in which the hams were cooked.

We used to take the threshing tackle down to Cotton Farm. We had to have seventeen big horses to pull the portable engine and the drum down Cotton Lane at Graveley Corner. There would be eleven horses belonging to Mr Farr and six horses borrowed from Mr Woods at Church Farm - eight pairs and one in front, which I used to lead. When we were going down the lane, the mud was so deep that the fire box on the engine was sliding along on the mud – and the wheels were sliding as well! We took the drum first, then the engine, then we came back and fetched the 'Jackstraw' and the chaff-cutter – then back home, after it had taken all day to finish the job.

One of my jobs was to drive plough for Mr Cullip, who was horse-keeper. He was a good weather forecaster. He studied the sun, the moon, the stars, the ark, the sky and the clouds – and many other things, and his forecasting was much more reliable than anything we are given today. When we were going out into the fields in the morning with the horses, Mr Cullip would say, "Bring your coat, boy. Red sky this morning, ploughboy's warning.' Crows on the grass were signs of rain and, if we heard Eltisley clock strike in the morning, it would rain before we came home. A circle round the moon was another sign of rain. On the other hand, he would say, "Evening red, morning grey, two good signs of a nice, fine day," or "The ark is pointing the right way for fine weather," and "The skylarks are getting up high, so it is going to be a nice day."

When we were in the fields with the horses in the summer-time and there was a thunder storm, we had to stand out in the rain and hold the horses until the storm was over. The horses were very frightened of thunder, so, if there was likely to be a storm, we always took our coats and a thick bag (or sack) to hang over us.

When the men were carting hay or clover, or in the harvest when they were carting peas, they had to use an elevator, which was driven by horse power. The horse went round and round, all day long. For days and days, I have just walked behind that horse with a little thin stick or whip to keep the horse going. If the horse stopped, the job would be at a standstill. It was very tiring for me, walking round and round, hour after hour – and it wasn't very nice for the horse either!

When the First World War broke out in 1914, I had just left school and started working for Mr Farr. Jim Currington, Tom Currington and I were dressing wheat with the old dressing machine and I was turning the handle. Tom Currington said that, when he was in the reading room the night before, he saw something in the paper that might interest me. He said he would cut it out and bring it back after lunch – which he did. I learned it off by heart and can still remember it. It goes like this:

I asked a girl to marry me, but she asked to be excused, so I excused her. Then I married her mother. Then my father married the girl. When I married the girl's mother, the girl became my daughter. And, when my father married the girl, the girl became my mother. So, if my father is my son and my daughter is my mother, who am I? My mother's mother, who is my wife must be my grandmother and I, being my grandmother's husband must be my own grandfather.

Tom Currington also told me he another tongue-twister he had seen in the paper:

Which switch is the switch, Miss, for Ipswich?
It's the Ipswich switch, which I require.
Which switch switches Ipswich? With this switch
You have switched my switch on the wrong wire.
You have switched me on to Northwich, not Ipswich,
And now to prevent further hitch,
If you will tell me which switch is Northwich and
Which switch is Ipswich, I will know which switch is which.

When walking across the fields to Caxton, the prettiest sight one could wish to see on a spring morning was eight teams of horses, three in each team, ploughing for Mr Hooley of Papworth Hall. The brasses on all the harnesses glittering in the sunshine. There was a harness room on each farm and one man in each doing nothing but oiling harness and shining the brasses – and every gate and fence on Mr Hooley's farms was painted white and kept in good condition too.

In 1913, I saw in the *St Neots Advertiser* that Yelling was having a new parson coming into Yelling Rectory. he was the Rev. Thomas Elms Fisher, a breezy Irishman. His wife was a German lady. In a very short time, the only congregation was the parson's wife – she was the bell ringer – and the parson preached to her. The congregation was 'on strike' because she was a German.

In 1914, I played my first game of cricket for the Yelling First Team against Croxton. I was 13 years old. My Uncle Jessie was captain and he put me in at number nine. As I was going out to the wicket, he said, "Sixpence if you carry your bat out," which I did, having scored ten runs. We knocked Croxton out and batted again.

Uncle Jessie said, "You'd better carry on where you left off and go in first with Sid Currington." I did, and we scored 72 runs before we parted. I was out when I hit a ball and we ran, but Perce Meeks picked up the ball and threw it straight into the stumps and ran me out. I had scored 15 runs. That added up to 25 runs for only once out – not a bad start to my cricketing career. In the evening, several of us lads were standing outside Miss Hedges' shop in Yelling when Mr Quick, the schoolmaster, came up and said, "Congratulations, Harold! I've been hearing big things about you today, and I'm very pleased." He went into the shop and, when he came out, he gave me a big bag of sweets, saying, "That is for what you have done today. Keep it up!" Although it is 78 years ago, I still remember all the Croxton team who played on that day – but, alas, they have all gone now.

The team was as follows:

Jess Saywell (who bowled the first ball to me. I can see it now, about six inches wide of my off stump), Bunny Sewell, Archie Sewell, Charlie Brace, Billy Brace, Herbert Brace, Mr Cousins, Joe Seymour, Alf Beal, Perce Meeks, Bill Flanders

From that day, I was opening bat for 40 years until I packed up, when I was 53 years old – not a bad run! At the end of my first season, the War broke out and, although we played a few games during the war, the Cricket Club closed down.

During the First World War, I played cricket for Papworth St Agnes, which I enjoyed very much. At one Papworth St Agnes Feast, they asked me if I could take a mate with me to play. I said, "Yes, I could. I would bring Roy Bartlett", who was an Australian soldier on leave next door to us. He had already asked me if I could get him some cricket. We walked across the fields and, as it was a lovely day, Mrs Sperling from Lattenbury Hall, some of her daughters and the gardener's wife, Mrs Arnold, brought tea tables, crocks and all the food on to the cricket field in the old donkey cart. There were also some sweet stalls. They put them close to the Meadow Plantation, which was used as the cricket field, near where the footbridge crosses the brook down Barnfield Lane. We had a really good game of cricket and a very nice tea – all free, given by Mr and Mrs Sperling, which we all enjoyed. When the cricket was finished, we all walked up to the village and sat around the little old bakehouse, where Fred Rossin served the beer through the little window at the end of the bakehouse. Then we spent the evening having a sing-song. The Australian thoroughly enjoyed it.

Roy Bartlett was a very good cricketer, so the next Saturday, when Yelling were playing at home in Mr John Green's field, I invited him to play for us. He said to me, "Harold, I like your batting very much, so I am going to bring my camera to take a photo of you batting, so I can take it back to Australia with me. I will let you get nicely going before I take the photo." When I had scored 24 runs, he came on the field and stood there with his camera, waiting for the bowler to bowl the next ball. When he delivered the ball and I made my stroke, he took my photo. As it happened, I was clean bowled! That was through thinking more about him than the bowler.

When I left school at 13 years old, we had to get to work at seven o'clock in the morning and work until five o'clock during the winter months. Then, on the first of March, we worked from six o'clock in the morning until half past five. During harvest time, we worked from five o'clock in the morning until seven o'clock in the evening. But if we worked with the 'Harvest Gang', who were working on a piece-work rate, we would work from five o'clock in the morning until nine thirty or ten o'clock at night.

After harvest, we would be ploughing right through the winter. There were three horses on each plough, walking one behind the other in the furrow. The boy driving the horses would have a line on the back horse's head, through a ring in the middle horse's halter and on to the front horse's head. The boy always carried a whip, so he could use it to make each horse 'pull his whack'. We would unhook the plough at 1.30 pm, so we could get home and ungear the horses to go for our dinner at 2 pm. After dinner, we sometimes carted straw to litter the yards with wheat straw, then fill the racks with barley straw for fodder. Or we would clean the stables out, clean and grind mangolds, or take horses to the blacksmith to be shod, or take harness to Billy Fields to be mended.

After a time, I had to be house boy. I cleaned the shoes and leggings and collected the eggs. There were hundreds of hens running about the yards and, at Dry Close, near Yelling Chapel, there were hens everywhere among the stacks. I often got a bucket full of eggs and took them to the farmhouse, then I went back to get another lot. Also at the farmhouse, there was a henhouse, which was full of fleas. My mother told me to tell Mrs Farr that I was not to go in there – which I did. Mrs Farr said I was not to worry about the fleas. She said, "When you have been in that henhouse, go straight into the stable for about ten minutes and all the fleas will leave you – because of the smell of the horses' urine."

Each year, at the beginning of June, I used to dig 12 shallow hollows in the ground and make nice nests with some short cavings. (Cavings were the short straws left under the threshing machine.) Into each nest I put 15 eggs – but I never used eggs which had been laid in May. I put a wooden coop over each nest, then I went and fetched some broody hens and I put one hen in each coop, pulled down the slide and covered the coop with a sack. Each afternoon, I took off the sack and lifted the slide, after I had put food outside the coop. The hens came out to feed, but I never let them be off the eggs for more than 20 minutes. I returned them to the coops, pulled down the slide and replaced the sacks. Sometimes I would catch two or three fowls and put them in the fattening pen for nine days – but no longer because they begin to lose weight after nine days. I also had to gather all the fruit from the orchard and store it.

When we were carting corn to St Neots, to the mill or the station with a wagon and four horses, I used to go with the horse keeper to mind the horses, while the men unloaded the corn. Sometimes, when that was done, we would load up with oil-cake or cotton-cake for the cattle, or maybe a load of coal. Then the horse keeper would pull up at a pub or The Station Hotel and have a pint of beer, which he was allowed whenever he went what we called 'teaming'. The boy who was with him was allowed a bottle of ginger beer.

During the journey, I used to count every car I saw from Yelling to St Neots and back again. Some days I counted only one, sometimes two or three, but one day I counted six cars and I was so excited that, when I got home, I rushed indoors to tell Mum, "I saw *six* cars today!" But that only happened once in a long, long time.

When the men on the farm were at muck cart, they were allowed one pint of beer each day and the boys driving cart were allowed a bottle of ginger beer. For threshing, the men were allowed two pints of beer and the boys two bottles of ginger beer. Hay cart was best, when men were allowed three pints of beer and the boys three bottles of ginger beer!

On Mr Main's farm at Toseland Manor, the men had beer every day, whatever job they were doing. One man did nothing else but take beer round to the other men with a pair of yokes and two two-gallon jugs – one on each side. Mr Main employed a lot of men. There was one named Abey Corn. Mr Main said to him, "Will you move that stone from the back door, Corn?" Corn said, "'Yes, Master." Later in the day, Mr Main said to him, "Did you move that stone, Corn?" And Corn said, "Yes, Master," which he had not done – and Mr Main knew it. Mr Main said, "Liar, Corn. Go to Hell, Corn. And be burned, Corn." And Corn said, "If I get there first, Master, I will make it bloody hot for you!"

Each year, when the harvest was over, the steam engines with their big old cultivator came in and fetched the fields up in great clods. When the fields had laid for a time, the horse keeper and I would go to scuffle, with four big horses to pull the scuffle. I led the two front horses and the horse keeper walked behind the scuffle.

Walking on those great big clods gave me a sweat-galled behind (which was inflammation caused by sweating and chafing) and I couldn't walk or ride because my behind was so painful. Old Maria Currington saw me hobbling about, hardly able to walk, and she said, "Whatever is the matter with you?" I told her about my painful behind and she said, "Go and look along the side of the roadway, past the old millhouse and you will see some silver leaves, flat on the ground, very much like fern leaves. They are called 'Tansy' leaves. Pick four or five of them and clap them between the cheeks of your old arse and they will soon cure that." I did as she told me – and it worked! Within an hour, I was playing cricket – and I have never suffered such inflammation from that day to this.

Then I was sent to High Hayden Farm as ploughboy – up and down the field every day. "Hail, rain, snow or blow, a-ploughing we must go!" Each day, I had an hour for dinner. As soon as I had finished eating my dinner, I would collect a bucketful of stones and tip them on the bank of the horse pond, which was full of rats. Then I dipped water out of the pond and tipped in the holes. The rats would jump into the pond and swim about in the water. When a dozen or so were swimming about on the pond, I started throwing at them with the stones I had tipped there. When I had killed that lot, I washed some more out and had another go. I must have killed hundreds. I did this every day – and I would throw as straight as I could shoot.

When Mr Cullip and I were Martin-cultivating (so-called because the cultivator was made by a firm called Martin) in Dicks Hedge Field at High Hayden Farm during the 1914-1918 war, I was leading the two front horses. The gamekeeper told me to keep a lookout for peewits' eggs and he would pay me two shillings and sixpence for each one I found. There was a great demand for them at that time. Two shillings and sixpence was a great deal of money in those days, so, while I was walking up and down the field, I kept my eyes on the ground and picked up quite a lot. When there was only one, two or three in the nest, I knew they were good, but, as soon as there were four or more in the nest, I knew it was too late. Three of them would be 'turned' and not fit to eat – and I could not tell which egg was the fourth one, which was fresh. Peewits' eggs always lay with the narrow ends pointing to the centre of the nest. A peewit only sits on its nest when the weather is dull. As soon as the sun shines, it will leave the nest and let the sun do the hatching. When I was a boy, a lot of peewits were caught in long nets, but I never did that kind of netting.

I did do other kinds of netting on most dark nights during the winter. Us lads carried a net on two poles, working along one side of the hedgerows and someone the other side of the hedge, with a pole, was hitting the hedge and driving the birds into the net. When the birds came into the net, whoever was carrying it closed the two poles together and lay it on the ground, took out the birds – then off we would go again.

When I was at Mr Farr's, we had three weeks threshing barley. The job I did was 'mind dress chaff'. (Minding dress chaff was hanging bags on the side of the threshing drum, where the barley hailes and any other rubbish that came off the barley kernels came out, and, when one of the bags got full, I took it off and replaced it with another.) I was smothered with barley hailes (spiky awns from the beard of the barley ears, which stuck to clothing, scratched the skin and were very irritating). After three weeks, I bought a bicycle and used it to ride to work the next Monday morning. When I got there, the boss said, "You go and mind dress chaff again, boy." "Can't one of the other boys have a go at it for a change?" I asked, "I've already had three weeks at it." The boss said, "If you can't do that, you know what you can do." I refused to do the job, so I got on my bike and went to see Mr Knight at Wintringham, and asked if he could give me a job. He agreed and told me that the threshing tackle would be coming in a few minutes, ready to start after dinner. He asked me to come up to the house for my dinner, which I did. After dinner, when we were ready to start threshing, Mr Knight said to me, "Will you mind dress chaff, boy?" and I said, "Yes." "How much do you want a week?" he asked. I said I ought to be worth three shillings and sixpence a week to start with, but he said, "I will give you three shillings a week to start with and, if you get on alright, I will give you another sixpence in two weeks' time." I had been getting three shillings a week, close to home, able to get home for all meals, but now I was cycling about six miles for the same amount of money and my mother had to pack food each day! But I took most of my packed food back home again, because at dinner times we went into the harness room, where there was a lovely fire, and ate all the food that was left over from Mr and Mrs Knight's table – a lot of it untouched. It was brought to us with jugs of hot tea.

When the war started on the 4th of August 1914, I went to work for Mr Anthony. One afternoon, I went with him to cut Mr John Green's grass in the top field beside the St Ives road. Mr Anthony's son, Ken, came with us. Mr Anthony said, "I will do the first round for you, then you can manage on your own." During that first time round, Ken and I walked behind the cutter knife. Ken was catching butterflies and he jumped in front of the knife to get one and caught his foot in the knife. It cut through his shoe and through his foot, so his heel was hanging down. When we got him out of the knife, Mr Anthony said, "My dear boy, you are a cripple for life now." We 'clawed' one of the horses out of the cutter and I jumped on its back and galloped to the farm. I harnessed the nag and told Mrs Anthony what had happened. She came with me in the buggy, up to the field and then Mr and Mrs Anthony took Ken to the hospital. He pulled through and was quite alright again.

On Saturdays, when I was working for Mr Anthony, I used to walk from Yelling, down Hail Lane, to Eynesbury Hardwick to fetch some cows or bullocks and bring them to Yelling for the weekend, driving them all on my own through Eynesbury and St Neots. On Monday mornings, I took them to St Ives Market. On the way, some of them would get into the fields. When it had been raining on the standing corn, I got soaking wet fetching them out and I had to stay in St Ives all day in my wet clothes. In case I had to take any animals home again, when I got to the market, they gave me a ticket to get a 'tuppenny pork pie' from The White Hart Hotel.

One morning, I took some bullocks to St Ives and one of them went up a path to a house and the door was open. It went in the house and the woman squealed and she drove it out – it had to back out, as it could not turn round!

When I had been at the market all day, there were times when Mr Ashcroft of Whitehall Farm, Croxton, bought some cows at the market and wanted me to drive them from St Ives to Croxton for him – for which he would pay me threepence. One day, he bought some and asked me to drive them to Croxton, so I said, "What are you going to pay me for it?" He replied that he would pay me threepence as usual – but I told him I would not do it for less than sixpence. He said he could not pay all that – so I did not take them.

At this time, when we went into St Ives, just over the level crossing there was a toll-gate, where we had to pay tuppence to a man sitting in a kind of sentry box. There was also a toll-gate at Wintringham, where we had to pay tuppence to a man who used to sit in the porch of a bungalow. The porch was also used by policemen. One, on his beat from St Neots, would meet one from Eltisley and they would sit there, talking in the porch. When I was working with Teddy Cole, he would say to me the next day, "Those blooming policemen kept me awake last night, sitting in our porch talking."

One Saturday afternoon, Mr Aubrey Anthony and I were cutting wheat for Mr John Green near what we called the Bottom Plantation. I said to Mr Anthony, "Look at these two planes flying in and out of that cloud." At that moment, they collided. One plane was from Yelling

Airfield and the other from Wyton. The two pilots were killed. One, from Yelling, whom I knew, was Lieutenant Pearce. I did not know the other one. That was in 1915, during the First World War.

Now back to another tale about Lieutenant Pearce from Yelling Airfield. On the Sunday before Lieutenant Pearce was killed the following Saturday, my uncle Jessie (who had lost his right leg during the First World War) and I went out for a walk. We had just assed the Toseland Manor and turned to come home, when we saw Lieutenant Pearce and Lieutenant Cowper go towards St Neots on a new Red-Indian motorbike. This was the first time on the bike and they were seeing how quickly they could go from Yelling Airfield to St Neots Market Square and back. On the way back, they were just passing my uncle and I, quite close to the manor where Mr Main lived. He had a white terrier, which was old and very steady and, just as the motorbike passed, it started crossing the road - just in front of them. As they tried to avoid hitting the dog, they caught the grass verge and crashed on the road, close to us. Lieutenant Cowper was riding the motorbike and Lieutenant Pearce was riding pillion, The crash threw Lieutenant Pearce over the top of Lieutenant Cowper, and the officer's cane which Lieutenant Pearce carried was smashed clean in half. I remember what Lieutenant Cowper said to us, when he picked himself up off the ground. He said, "Well, what with crashes in bloody aeroplanes and now on motorbikes, I am doing fine." (A plane he was flying a few days before had crashed in the field close to The Spread Eagle, Croxton, opposite the petrol station.) But his luck did not hold, and he was killed in his plane the following Saturday.

About the same time, on a Saturday afternoon, a light aircraft took off from St Ives common and hit the steeple of St Ives church and completely knocked it off. A number of Boy Scouts were either in the church or the churchyard at the time, but I don't think anyone was injured. Several of us lads cycled over to St Ives the next day to see the damage.

Writing about St Ives reminds me about one Monday, when I was taking a great big bull to the market in a float. The bottom of the float was near the ground and it had high sides and front. The bull was very large – it weighed a ton – and it had a chain around its neck, which was fixed to the float. On my way to St Ives, the bull jumped up and got its front legs over the front of the float where I was sitting. I soon jumped off, because the bull was laying on its stomach, half in and half out of the float. I kept wondering what was going to happen next, but I got it to market safe and sound – and they gave me a ticket to go to The White Hart to get my 'tuppenny pork pie'.

In 1915 two policemen were sent down from Bethnal Green, London, to work on the land. Their names were Bill Moore and Bob Hunter. They were working on the farm at the top end of Yelling which, before the war, was owned by Mr John Green. The two policemen were lodging with us at New Zealand, which was at the other end of the village. One day, they were going back to work after dinner and they asked me to go back with them, and to take my two-two rifle with me, as there were a lot of rabbits on the farm. As we passed Yelling church, and were going past the first house on the right, which was owned by Mr Walter Norman, one of the policemen said to me, "I bet you couldn't put a bullet through the weathercock on the top of the church." Being quite a lad of only 14 years, I was thrilled to have a go, which I did – and the bullet went straight through the weathercock! The policeman said, "That was a fluke. I bet you couldn't do it again," so that tempted me to have another shot. The second shot went through, close beside the first shot – and you can see the holes quite plainly to this day.

My father had a gang of men digging drains for Sir Douglas Newton. There was a draining competition at Great Gransden and Sir Douglas asked my father to go to it – all expenses paid. So my father agreed to go, and he won first prize. Next day, Sir Douglas went to my father and said, "Congratulations, Meeks. I knew you would win it, that's why I wanted you to go." Then Sir Douglas put a gold sovereign into my father's hand – and that was in addition to the day's expenses! The next year, in 1916, the competition was held at Longstowe. Once again my father entered and again my father won first prize. That was the last competition ever held.

During the First World War, there was a Belgian refugee living in Yelling. His name was M. Dalaraat and he wanted to come round the fields with us, so we let him have a pole to hit the hedge. Sometimes he would hear a robin chirp when disturbed, and the Belgian would shout, "Neir, neir, lister, lister!" because he knew it was a robin.

Sometimes we went round the haystacks, strawstacks, also buildings and houses with ivy growing on the walls – because they would be full of sparrows. Some of the women in the village were fond of sparrow, linnet or blackbird pie, so they would buy the birds from us. Sparrows at three a penny, green linnets at the same price and blackbirds at a penny each. This was done on dark evenings. When it was moonlight, we went round the hedgerows with our catapults or air guns to shoot all the sparrows we could. That pleased the farmers, because the sparrows did a lot of damage to the crops. On wet evenings, we went into the hovels, sheds and barns, where the sparrows were roosting. One of us had a pole and another a torch. The one with the pole poked out the sparrows and the one with the torch shone it on the wall – it was best in a corner. He also had a stick and, as the sparrows flew out of their roosting places, they flew towards the light and were hit by the stick. This suited the farmers.

During the First World War Mr Fyson of Warboys went to quite a number of garden fetes, dances on lawns, and so on, with what he called his 'V.C. Cockerel', which he would put up by auction, to raise money for the Red Cross. He would stand out on the lawns, when the dancing had stopped, with the cockerel perched on his forefinger, put it up for auction, knock it down to the highest bidder – then start all over again, then again and so on, as long as he could keep getting bidders. Mr Fyson must have raised hundreds of pounds for the Red Cross, but he still kept the cockerel!

One morning, I was at plough with Teddy Cole the horse keeper, and I told him, "They are going to build an aerodrome in Yelling." He laughed and said, "Wherever did you get that tale from? They will never build an aerodrome at Yelling." Soon after I had told him, Mr Knight said, "Yes, that is right, Cole. In fact, they have started on it already." Teddy said, "I couldn't believe it when Harold told me." I think this was in July 1915.

When the aerodrome was in operation, I used to take milk, cream, eggs and butter each day to the officers. Then I collected the swill for the pigs every Sunday. Every evening in the summer, there were hundreds of people down the Croxton road, packed as thick as they could stand to watch the flying. The planes swooped low over their heads and I saw a number of women faint and they had to be taken home. Some would squeal. On Sunday morning, they were practising firing rockets off the wing, four on each plane wing – firing them into the ground. They had about 18 inches of explosive and a long stick – about seven feet long. They fired them over the Croxton road into the aerodrome. My mate and I were standing on the road when one rocket fell short and stuck in the ground close to us. They also practised bomb dropping. The target was a white sheet, about seven feet square, in the corner of the aerodrome, near George Brittain's and Mr Joe and Owen Farr's boundary and the Croxton Estate boundary. One day, I picked up the nose cap of one of the bombs and took it on to the road, where there were a lot of people who wanted to see it. One chap said, "I will give you one shilling an sixpence for it" – so I let him have it.

One morning, I saw smoke coming from the aeroplane hangars, which were on fire and soon after the airfield closed down and my job taking milk, butter, eggs and cream every day for the officers was finished. One day, when I took the milk, the officer's cook said, "We shan't be wanting any more this week Harold, as the place is closing down." The cook was a German, whose name was Mr Sadler. When the airfield closed down, he went into lodgings at the New Inn in St Neots High Street. he asked me to call in and see him when I was down on a Saturday evening, which I did.

He told me that he had got another job – painting the airship hangars at Cardington. He said what a good job it was and jolly good money and he asked me, "Why don't you come over there? You will get a good job." So on the Friday before Whit-Monday, another chap and I went over to Cardington and saw Mr Sadler busy painting, so we went up to him and he said, "There is the foreman, go and see him." We did so and asked about a job and he said, "Yes, you can start on Tuesday morning, after the holiday at eight o'clock." He told us what the pay was and it suited us fine – there was no such pay down our way. We went to Cotton End, Bedford, and got lodgings, so that was OK. Then the very next day, Mr John Woods of Church Farm, Yelling, offered my mate a job on the farm, close to his home. When he came and told me, I said, "Well, I shan't go on my own" – so that was that.

The winter of 1916 was a sharp one. We had eight weeks of frost and snow, and there was skating on Mr Anthony's horse pond for eight weeks – all February and March. On Tuesday, 28th March, 1916, there was the worst blizzard ever known. There were more than a thousand trees down on the Rowley Estate, St Neots. The day after the blizzard, several of us walked over to Croxton to see the road blocked, all the way from The Spread Eagle to Eltisley, by fallen telegraph wires and trees. In Yelling also, trees were falling everywhere and the snow was drifting, five or six feet deep in places. When my brother Buller and I were coming home, down the village between Yelling Chapel and New Zealand, we saw something sticking out of the snow drift. When we got to it, to our surprise, we found it was Charlie Dawborn. He had fallen in the ditch and, because the ditch was filled with snow, he could not get out. All we could see was his head. I'm sure that, if we hadn't come along, he would have been buried, because he would not have been able to get out on his own. My brother and I pulled him out and he was alright.

In 1916, my uncle Jessie was very friendly with a chap from Croxton whose name was Joe Flinders. Joe was a proper lad – and, like Jessie, had lost a leg in the war. One Thursday, we all went down to St Neots market and decided to go and have a drink and a game of billiards in the New Inn in the High Street. When we had finished and were just leaving, an Australian soldier who had just came in said, "You chaps had better have a drink with me before you go." He asked me what I would like and, as it was a rather cold morning, I said, "I will have a drop of rum." He asked my uncle, "What's yours?" and Uncle said, "I will have a drop of rum as well." Then he asked Joe Flinders what he would like and Joe replied, "I will have a double rum and a large packet of Gold Flake (meaning cigarettes)." When we got outside, I said, "You've got a nerve on you, Joe." He said, "What? They get the money, so why not make them spend it?" I have a laugh whenever I think about that incident, although it is 76 years ago.

While I was working for Mr Knight, the steam ploughing engines ploughed a 30-acre rough-grass field very deeply, in great big furrows. After it had laid for a time, Teddy Cole, who was horse keeper, and I went with four horses and a cultivator to move those furrows. I was leading the front horses and, as we were going along, I noticed rabbits sitting in the furrows, so I told Teddy Cole and he crept on his hands and knees and grabbed hold of them. From then on, I kept watching for them and saying, "Here's another one, Ted!" When we went back to our yard at dinner time, we had 26 rabbits hanging on the horses' aims. Mr Knight saw and said, "Wherever have you been getting them from, Cole?" Cole replied, "They were sitting between the furrows, Master." Mr Knight asked if there were any more and Cole said, "You can bet your life there are, as we have got all these from the ground we have moved today." Mr Knight said he would go and fetch Walter (that was my father) and they would go and walk the rest of the field. They did so, and shot 76 more rabbits – that was 102 rabbits altogether off that one field.

In that same field, three years later, my brother Charlie, Sid Webb and I were carting clover and I was on top of a very high load. I said, "Give me one more forkful each." Sid Webb said, "Hold tight," and he poked the horse under the stomach with his fork. The horse reared up and stood on its hind legs, throwing me on to the hard ground. All I can remember was my brother Charlie saying, as they picked me up, "He's a 'dunner,' Sid."

Horses' aims were fitted into the horses' collar. Some were brass, some were iron and some were wood. When a horse was going into a cart, I put the aims on to the horse's collar, which had got what we called 'shoulder chains' to hook on to the cart shafts for the horse to pull the cart along. When the horse was going into chains, I put the aims on to the collar which had hooks on instead of chains. When the aims were strapped on to the collar, the tops of the aims stuck up about eight or nine inches above the collar – so we could hang whatever we liked on them.

When I was working for Mr Knight of Wintringham, I worked with Teddy Cole, the horse keeper. He told me that the threshing tackle had just been to Mr Houghton's on Tythe Farm, near St Neots Station. He said that, when they were threshing on that farm, the men were all allowed a pint of beer each. And he told me this tale.

One day, the engine driver went to the farmhouse to fetch the beer and they asked him how many men wanted beer. He said, "Well, there is old Bill Blowfield and his mate" – Bill Blowfield and his mate did not drink beer! – so that was two pints. Then he said, "And two engine men" – that meant the same two men – so that was four pints. Then he said, "There are two chaps who follow us around" so that was six pints. (Those two men didn't drink beer either!) Poor old Teddy Cole used to laugh about that.

While I was working with Teddy Cole, my hands were covered with warts. He said, "Would you like me to get rid of them for you?" I replied that I wished he would. He asked me to count how many I had, and he would write it on a card when he went home at lunch-time. He said, "They will all disappear and you won't miss them." One day, he said to me, "How are your warts?" I looked and said, "They are all gone." He asked, "Didn't you miss them?" I said, "No, I didn't know they had gone." He said, "I told you you wouldn't know when they went."

When I was working for Mr Knight and the steam engines and cultivators came in, we had to fetch water for them from Brookside Street, St Neots, just outside Mr Williamson's Cycle Shop – number eight, on the corner. The pump stood there all day and night, perhaps for a week or more. We pulled up there with the horses and huge water carts and, by hand, we had to pump them full of water. We had to get cracking or else we heard the engine whistles begin 'blowing for water'. When I go round that corner now, I often think to myself, "Whatever would happen these days if there was a large pump, two large horses and great big water carts standing there on the corner, several times each day and taking up most of the road?"

I think it was at this time that Rene Seymour from Croxton worked at Mr Knight's in the cowshed. She used to help with the milking, which was all done by hand. We were the same age – both born on the same day. We cycled home together each day, as far as The Spread Eagle. One day, she came to me and said, "I have got to go home now. My father (Bill Seymour) has fallen off a load of wheat, just down the Toseland road, and has been killed." The horse, which was being led by Ern Saywell, had stumbled and Mr Seymour had been thrown down on to the road.

One day, when I had been pigeon shooting on Mr Thomas Hawkey's land at Wintringham, on the field near the Fox-holes, I was on my way home in Hail Lane, near Weald Corner, where I saw two Gypsy blokes. They had got a lovely fire and, as it was very cold, I stayed with them round the fire for quite a while. They had a dirty old can, full of boiling water, hanging over the fire. All the time I was there, they kept on pulling stinging nettles and putting them into the can of water. When the nettles had been in the water for a time and were boiling, they both had a dirty old mug each, which they kept filling out of the old can that was over the fire. They kept on saying, "That's lovely. Would you like some?" but I kept saying, "No, thank you." They said, "You would never have any boils or pimples if you got plenty of this nettle tea down you" – but I didn't fancy it!

There was a big elm tree standing at the top of the field, right in the corner, where Mr David Hawkey's land joined Donaldson's. There was a strand of barbed wire on that tree and a blackbird built its nest on the wire, where it was fastened to the tree. There was a thunderstorm one day when the blackbird was sitting on its nest. The tree was struck by lightning, killing the blackbird. After the storm, the blackbird was still sitting on the nest, as if it was alive. The lightning did not go down to the ground, as the tree was not marked any lower than the barbed wire – so I think it must have travelled along the wire.

When I worked on that farm, whenever a horse was taken into the fields, we always had to take a nosebag for the horse, so, when we were having our food, the horse could do the same.

Mr Knight, my employer, came to me one Saturday morning and asked me to have a go at the pigeons on the field next to Mr Rowley's narrow plantation. He asked me to come to the house and have some dinner, which I did, then I went to the field. When I got there, old Jack Ramply was there. He was a real old pigeon shooter. He asked me if I had come to have a go at the pigeons and, when I said, "Yes," he enquired whether I shot them flying, and I told him that I shot them in the trees. He said, "You have a go at them flying – you will like it much better. I will make your hide for you and let you do the shooting – but I will tell you when to shoot." So he put out the decoys and stood behind me in the hide. After a few minutes, one pigeon came and he told me to wait until he told me to shoot. He said, "Shoot," and I fetched it down. He said, "Well done. That was as well as I could have done it." While he was with me, I shot 28 pigeons. From then on, I had open hides and shot pigeons flying, which I liked much better.

Then I left Mr Knight's, as I heard that they were setting folk on in the munition works at Luton, and the money was much better then on the farms. Fred Stocker, George Leach and I cycled to Luton and tried every munition works in Luton (and there were quite a lot), but the first thing everyone asked was "How old are you?" When we said, "Seventeen years," as we were all the same age, then the answer was always, "No, because, as soon as you get used to the job, you will be called up for the army." We then went to the bomb factory in Dunstable Road, but, as we arrived, the workers were just coming out, and they were all as yellow as buttercups – so we did not try there!

At that time, I had three brothers fighting in France and my Uncle Jessie, who lived with us, had just been wounded and, as it was getting near my calling up age, they all said to me, "For God's sake, keep out of the army, if you possibly can." So I joined the navy in 1918. I passed everything and they told me they would be calling me up in a few days – but I haven't heard anything from that day to this – and I signed on for 12 years!

I had two weeks' holiday while I was waiting to hear from the navy, but, when we didn't hear from them, I got a job at Papworth Everard, working for Mr Thackray of Huntingdon. The foreman was Alf Peacock. Dr Verrier-Jones had taken over Papworth Hall to make it into a sanatorium. I worked on the Hooley's Cricket Pavillion to turn it into a recreation room. I also helped to turn the coal place into a laundry. Alf Foster and I erected all the huts for the patients – a long row of them reaching from the cricket pavillion down to the hall. While we were working there, Papworth Wood was cut down. The tree trunks were carted away and the branches left behind. The wood was full of rabbits, which sat under the branches. I had a little .22 pistol with a barrel of 12 or 14 inches long, so I used it with both hands. The foreman would say, "Harold, go and get us all a rabbit or two," which I did with no trouble at all. I was in the wood, shooting rabbits, when the church bells started to ring and all the factory hooters began to blow, telling us that the war was over. It was a nasty November day with fog and drizzle.

When the First World War ended, I cycled to St Neots, where the people of St Neots had made a great big bonfire and were dancing and enjoying themselves. While I was there, I felt that killer flu coming on.

I had ten weeks in bed, with Dr Harrison coming in to see me twice a day for some time. There were over four million people who died with that terrible flu in this country.

In 1919, I went round the village to see if there was anyone who would like to help me restart the Cricket Club. I had quite a good response, and we got the Club going again in five weeks. Our first match was Soldiers v Civilians. The Civilians had a very good win. I know I scored 35 runs. All that season, we played friendlies, but the next year (1920) saw the beginning of the 'Christmas League.' Abbotsley won it the first year and Yelling were runners-up. Then Yelling won it for the next three years running, missed a year, then won it a couple of times more. For several years, I played for the St Neots Tuesday team, where Ernie Albone was captain. I also played for Waresley and District in the Smith Barry Cup. I played for Great Paxton a few times too in the Smith Barry Cup and, at most village feasts, I played for two or three days for various clubs.

I played at Eltisley Feast on the Green. Frank Rawlins, the Bedfordshire opening bat, and I were playing together, when George Rose was bowling his fastest. A ball kicked up and hit Frank Rawlins on the head and he fell to the ground as if he had been shot. A doctor and nurse, who had been watching the cricket, rushed on to the pitch, cut the hair round the wound and put a dressing on it. Then they took him straight to the hospital. It was a very nasty gash.

I also got a nasty one from George Rose, when I was playing against him on St Neots Common, but my gash was under the chin, and it put me flat on my back, as he was bowling very fast at that time. In a few seconds, I was drenched in blood – and I still carry the scar.

I got another nasty one when I was playing Married v Single and my brother-in-law was bowling. The ball kicked up and hit me in the mouth, knocking my teeth out and smashing my jaw – it put me in bed for weeks.

Soon after that, we started a cricket club in Toseland. The first year, we joined the Cranfield League, Second Division, and we won it. We then had to go into the First Division, which was run in two sections. Brampton were winners of one section, and they hadn't lost a game.

Toseland were winners of the other section – and we hadn't lost a game, so we played Brampton in the Final on Buckden's ground. We had quite a good game – which we won.

In those days, when we finished the cricket, the two teams would all go to the village pub and spend an enjoyable evening, drinking and having a sing-song. This would happen whether we were playing at home or away. The two teams stayed together until the pub closed. Then the visiting team would set off for home on their cycles, with bats, pads, etc., and still wearing their whites – a happy end to an enjoyable day.

There were five Meeks brothers in the Yelling team at one time – Charlie, Buller, Harold, Stan and Reg, with Tom Leach, Fred Leach, Sid Currington, Walter Currington, Tommy Reed and Perce Reed. We had a very strong team and, for two or three seasons, the only man to score over 20 runs against us was Jack Mahoney of The Spread Eagle, Croxton. Playing at Croxton, he scored 24 runs. That was the highest score made against us for several years.

Waresley came to Yelling one Saturday, and we batted first. We scored 46 and Waresley scored 46 for seven wickets at tea-time. When my brother Charlie and I left the field for tea, Oscar Sharp, who was captain of Waresley said, "Well, we have never had the pleasure of beating Yelling before, but I'm pleased to say we shall have that pleasure today." My brother Charlie said, "The game is not finished yet, Mr Sharp." Oscar Sharp said, "Surely we can score one run to win, with three wickets in hand." But they didn't get that one run – we got those three wickets, without them scoring, so the game ended in a draw.

In September 1919, the Croxton Estate was alive with rabbits. Mr Fairy, who was estate manager, asked my brother Buller if he would do the rabbit catching, and he agreed. Buller asked me to go with him, but there were more rabbits than he could cope with, so Buller and my brother Charlie went together and I went with Reg Cawthorne, the head keeper's son. We killed over twenty thousand rabbits that year. When we finished rabbiting at the end of March, I went to work for Mr Wrycroft at St Neots, building the four houses near the telephone box at Yelling. I told Mr Wrycroft that I would be leaving him in

September, as we had promised to do the rabbiting again on the Croxton Estate. We killed over twenty thousand again in the 1920-1921 season.

During the shooting season, when Sir Douglas Newton had the main shoots, they killed between 1000 and 1200 head each day, the first day on the North Lodge side of the A45 and the next the other side. After the shoot, Reg Cawthorne and I did the picking up. We often picked up as many as 50 pheasants and, many a time, I climbed to the tops of the trees to get the pheasants that were lodged there. When the pheasant shooting was finished, Sir Douglas Newton would have a day rabbit shooting. We would follow up behind, ferreting. Often, we would find a hole full of rabbits. The last one had been shot and all the rest had suffocated. One day, we had 27 in one hole, 17 in another and 11 in another – all dead. In each case, the last one had been shot.

One Saturday, I was walking the fields from Abbotsley Brook on the Red Hill towards the South Lodge plantation beside Sir Douglas and Lady Newton – that was before they were made Lord and Lady Eltisley. It was all grassland at that time and the rabbits were sitting about all over the place. We had already run the long nets out down the side of the plantation and, as we were walking, I said, "There is a rabbit sitting just in front, Sir Douglas." He said, "Where, Meeks? Show me." I tried to show him the rabbit, but he just could not see it. He said to Lady Newton, "Come here, Muriel. Can you see a rabbit sitting in front," but she couldn't see it either. "Neither can I," said Sir Douglas, "I don't think there is one." I disagreed and insisted that there was a rabbit there. Sir Douglas said, "Well, let's put it up then," which we did. He fired both barrels at it and missed – although he was usually a very good shot. He said, "That was very bad shooting, wasn't it, Meeks?" but I didn't answer, only smiled and we walked on a bit further. There was another rabbit sitting in front, once again I told Sir Douglas, once again he could not see, neither could Lady Newton. "Here, Meeks, take my gun and see what you can do," said Sir Douglas. His gun was a single trigger gun of a kind I had never fired before. He said, "Put the rabbit up, Meeks, and give it a sporting chance," which I did. I fired, and the rabbit rolled over and over for about ten yards. "Good shot," said Sir Douglas, "that's not the first rabbit you have shot, Meeks, but you must have a wonderful eye."

It was in 1920 when the head gamekeeper's son on the Croxton Estate, Reg Crawthorn, and I were rabbitting together. We did not see each other again until January 1986. I went to see him at his home in Histon after 66 years and we talked about the good old times we spent together. I mentioned the two spaniels which we had picking up after the shoots – and he fetched out photographs of them both, which brought back many more memories.

Many a time, when a rabbit jumped up and was shot, another one rolled out of a form and got killed by the same shot – two killed with one shot. When we were ferretting, on a frosty morning, and the long grass was white with rime, we could see patches of grass with no rime on – and we knew that there was a rabbit under each patch. My brother Buller and I walked to each rime-less patch, carrying our catapults, and, as we walked round these patches, we could see a little round hole in the heap of grass and the rabbit's head showing. We could hit them on the head almost every time – it was not very often we missed, so we could have quite a good heap of rabbits before we even started ferretting.

I have heard some folk say they have got lovely, big ferrets for rabbiting. They can have their big ferrets – give me the smallest ferrets I can get. They can get past the rabbits and, if they get hold of a rabbit, they are unable to hold it. With small ferrets, there is not so much digging because the rabbits will bolt. But you do need a bigger ferret if you have to dig – to pull the line along. In any rough place, where we could not net the holes, we would either bolt the rabbits and shoot them as they came out, or we would stink them out. Then they could sit out in the fields and we would walk the fields and shoot them. If a ferret laid up in a hole, we would take a piece of straw out of the ferret box, then take the inside out of a rabbit, wrap it inside the straw and place it in one of the holes, then block all the holes up. When we went back in the morning, the ferret would be curled up in the straw, asleep.

Many a time, when I have been ferreting, I have pulled out a rabbit, then put my hand into the hole again – and pulled out a rat. One time, near Dumptilow Farm, I pulled five rabbits and five big rats out of one burrow. Quite a number of times, when we have been ferreting, we have had two rabbits in one net at the same time. When we were out

Date.	November 10th	November 11th	1921		Pts.	Phs.	Hares	Rabs.	Wood cock.	Wild Duck.	Var.	TOTAL	BEAT.
No. Guns.	Seven	Seven											
	GUNS.	GUNS.		GUNS.									
	Kenneth Foster Esqr	Right Hon: Sir A. Boscawen MP			1	457	17	12	-	-	1	483	Elladys & Too Logs
	Philips Foster Esqr	Kenneth Foster Esqr											
	Earl of Kintorre	Earl of Kintorre											
	Sir Douglas Hairston	Sir Douglas Hairston			3	531	13	8	-	1	4	610	Gorse & North Lodge
	Right Hon: Major O'Neill MP	Basil Hairston Esqr											
	The Lord Stafford	Right Hon: Major O'Neill MP											
	Beaufort Whitmann Esqr	The Lord Stafford											
					4	1038	30	20	-	1	5	1095	GRAND TOTAL

ferreting, we always filled in the holes as we went, then, when we finished, we would come round to where we started and begin all over again. If the filled-in holes were open, then we would put a ferret in again. If the holes were still filled in, we knew there were no rabbits in there. Several times, when snaring rabbits, I have caught two rabbits in one snare – one round the neck and the other round its legs. One day, when my brother and I were ferreting along the Abbotsley Brook, the airship R26 came over – that was in 1919. (I also saw the airship 101, when it made its maiden flight just after 10 o'clock one summer evening – I think it was in 1920. And I remember quite well the Saturday night when it crashed in France – that was on 5th October 1930.)

In 1921 we moved from New Zealand in the Western end of Yelling, to Friends Farm, which my father farmed for 16 years. The summer was very hot and everywhere was dried up: there was no water in Toseland or Yelling. Toseland folk fetched water from the river and Yelling farmers fetched water from a pond on Friends Farm. The pond was continually filled from a spring on Hill Farm land (owned by Mr Sperling) called Nil Well. It never stopped flowing and each side of the stream the ground was almost red, owing to the iron the water contained. When I was a boy, I remember the doctor sending patients there to drink the water as a cure for rheumatism. During the hot summer of 1921, that well supplied water for most of the cattle in the village.

While we were living at New Zealand, all our drinking water had to be carried from a pump in White Pond Close – which is now Yelling Cricket Field. Us boys could carry only one bucket of water, but, if the men fetched it, they would take two buckets, wearing a yolk, which fitted on their shoulders. They had a small piece of board floating on top of the water, in each bucket, to prevent the water overflowing.

During 1921, Mr Knight of Wintringham Hall came to see my brother Buller, to ask him if he would dig a certain number of early potatoes each day for him, also so many bunches of red beetroot, and bunches of carrots. Beetroot were to have six beet in a bunch, carrots were to have 12 in a bunch and potatoes were to have 56 lbs in a bag. My brother and I took on the job and got two more chaps to help us – they were Billy Peak and Tom Leach. One morning, when we were about to have lunch, we picked up our food bags, but, when Billy Peak picked his bag up, a huge rat jumped out. It had gnawed a hole through the cloth in which his food was wrapped and had eaten part of his food. He threw the rest of it away – and we all three shared our lunch with him.

In September 1921, my brother Charlie heard that Mr Sperling of Lattenbury Hall was going to sell his rabbiting, so we went to see him about them. My brother and I bought them from him – and that season, we killed 8,786 rabbits! A lot of them were black and sandy-coloured ones. The next two or three years, Mr Churton of St Ives hired the shooting and sub-let the rabbiting to us during that time.

Captain Kendall told us this story, when he was rabbiting with us. He was the captain of a ship that was on its way to Canada, when he became suspicious of a man and a girl on the ship. He contacted Scotland Yard by Morse code and told them he thought he had Dr Crippen and Miss LaNeve on his ship. Scotland Yard told him to turn his ship around and come back to Liverpool, where they were waiting, and the couple were arrested. Dr Crippen murdered his wife in 1910.

One day, Captain Kendall was with us, when we were ferreting around the old moat of the Manor Farm at Papworth St Agnes, when a rabbit came out and sat outside the hole. The captain shot it and, when I picked up the rabbit, the ferret lay there dead, too. He had killed both rabbit and ferret with one shot.

In those days, a rabbit made a good meal for people with large families and was quite cheap. There were some places where we could sell rabbits for two shillings each, and the skins were worth one shilling and sixpence. That made a very cheap meal.

When we were ferreting round a pond at Dumptilow Farm, we had all the holes netted except one – and that one was two feet under water. Five rabbit came out of that hole and swam about in the pond. When they reached the banks, our little Jack Russell terriers were waiting for them – and they knew their jobs as well as we did. They knew every movement about ferreting, and anywhere along a brook bank, where we could not net, the terriers would sit on the bank, behind a stump with just one eye showing, so they could see when a rabbit was coming. They didn't often miss one. When hunting in a hedgerow, one ran 30 or 40 yards in front and sat in the middle of the hedge to kill every rabbit that ran along in front, while we were hunting along the hedge with the other terriers. When we reached her, she would come out of the hedge and run forward about the same distance again. We didn't need a gun – she would catch almost every rabbit that went along. Those terriers were worth their weight in gold. If you are kind to a dog, that dog will do its job well for you. Sometimes, when we were ferreting along a bank, holes ran out into a field, sometimes for six or seven yards, and those terriers would mark the spot where the rabbits lay – and that saved us a lot of digging!

When we first bought the rabbiting, we were troubled by poachers. One night, my brother Charlie was down at the Meadow Plantation, waiting for poachers and I was near Papworth Rectory, waiting. It was a very dark night and I stood in the middle of some green ash branches, beside the orchard. I heard sticks cracking and branches moving. I thought, "Here comes some trouble," but I stood still and several chaps (I think there were five of them) came close to me, and I could have touched any one of them. They were not poachers – they were after the apples and they filled their baskets and left. They never knew I was standing so close to them and I did not know who they were.

When we first bought the rabbiting, my brother Charlie and I were out without ferrets. Oliver Arnold, who was keeper and gardener for Mr Sperling, told us he had got four young ferrets we could have – but they hadn't done any work and did not know what a rabbit was! We bought the ferrets and went down the Meadow Plantation, beside the Huntingdon road and picked just one ferret to put in one hole. We heard a noise, so we knew there was a rabbit in there. But the ferret came out – so we put all four of the ferrets in the hole. Again, they all came out. We then put our nets down over some large burrows, but nothing happened. I was sure there was a rabbit in the first hole we tried, so I decided to dig the hole out. I hadn't dug far, when I felt in the hole and pulled a rabbit out, then another, and six more – making eight altogether. Then we took out our pocket knives and cut out the eyes of one of the rabbits and gave them to the ferrets. When they got the taste of blood, they worked well, and we had no more trouble. All four turned out to be really good ferrets, and that day we finished up with 76 rabbits, which we carried home across the fields to Yelling. My brother Charlie, who was as strong as an elephant, carried 50 and I carried 26 – and they hung very heavy by the time we arrived home! But never again!

Next day, we went to St Neots and saw old Mr Wren the fishmonger and made an arrangement with him to collect the rabbits every day from Papworth with his horse and cart. He paid us one shilling and threepence each.

When rabbiting or rat-catching, we always poured a few drops of turpentine in our hands and rubbed it over the ferret's body – that made the rabbits or rats bolt much quicker!

When we started ferreting in the park at Lattenbury, we began against the road, beside the arable field. There were lovely burrows all the way and, as it was the first time over, we couldn't understand why we could not find any rabbits. But about 80 yards from the road, while we were still netting all the holes, a stoat bolted out of the hole. From there, the holes were full of rabbits. That stoat had been through all the other holes we tried and had driven all the rabbits out.

One day, when I had been ferreting on my own, I was on my way home, walking along the grass field beside Barnfield Lane. Along the footpath, there were a number of cows with a bull in the field. They were quite a long way from me, when I heard a lumbering noise. I looked round and saw the huge bull coming at full speed. I was carrying 26 rabbits on a rope over my shoulder, a ferret box, my food bag and some nets. I tried to get to the gate but, when I saw I wasn't going to make it, I went towards the barbed-wire fence and dived headlong into it, with the bull close behind me. I got my head through the fence and I hung there, with my head down and the rabbits hanging all round my neck – and my feet up in the air! The ferret box was wedged in the wire and I was looking between my legs at the bull. He was scratching the ground with his front feet and the froth was running from his nose and his mouth. He was standing about four feet from me – and I could not move. After about ten minutes, the bull went back to the cows. I had great difficulty getting out of the barbed-wire. The blood was running out of my legs and arms, where the barbed-wire had cut me and my clothes were badly torn.

The next morning, I told the foreman what had happened the afternoon before. He said, "That bull won't hurt you – he is as quiet as a lamb." I replied, "I don't think so, Mr Walker." "Well," said he, "I am going to let him out again when I get home." Apparently he did so, because, as he walked across the yard, the bull went for him, tossed him up in the air and hurt him badly. I heard that he had broken arms and ribs and was taken straight to hospital. Mr Munns was sent for and the bull was killed. When Mr Walker recovered and returned home, he said, "I wish I had taken notice of what you told me, Harold."

Another time, my uncle Jessie and I were ferreting along the brook down Barnfield Lane beside the road. We had the ferrets under a big old tree and we thought we had all the holes netted, but a rabbit bolted out from under the tree and got away. I told my uncle there must be another hole under there somewhere and, to have a better look, I got hold of a branch and hung down over the brook bank. The branch broke and I fell into the brook, where the water was very deep and I was soaked all over. I walked from there, near the Huntingdon road, all the way to Yelling – and it was snowing and freezing hard. When I got home, I took all my clothes off, and they were frozen as hard as boards – they stood upright on their own! Because of that, I had a fortnight in bed!

My uncle, Jessie Meeks, had been in France with the 7th Bedfordshire Regiment in 1916, and was in the trenches with two more chaps and a Lewis gun. They heard the Germans talking a few yards away. My uncle got up out of the trench to have a look – and he told us that the Germans stood as thick as they could stand in the trenches. He got back into his trench and told his two mates to hand him the Lewis gun as he got up again out of the trench, which they did. He said that he mowed the Germans down like anyone mowing corn. Then he was shot in the arm and the knee. He crawled into a shell-hole and he laid there for 29 hours before he was picked up. Gangrene had set in and his right leg had to be amputated. He had 13 operations, but he never could wear an artificial leg, so he always used crutches. He eventually died of appendicitis when he was 38.

One day, we were carting clover up at Watland Field and my father was just finishing the stack when a heavy thunderstorm came over and it poured with rain. The belt on the petrol engine and the elevator kept coming off, so Arthur Baker was holding it on the engine wheel, George Bishop was holding it on the elevator and I was holding it in between the two. A flash of lightning came and ran round the two wheels. It paralysed both their hands and arms – but it didn't touch me!

One Saturday, about two o'clock, my brother and I had just finished our dinner down beside the road (the A45, where the new by-pass now begins) when a balloon came very low over the road near us. The rope was dragging on the road. Then the men threw out the anchor as the balloon passed Love's Farm, and it caught in the top of an ash tree. It pulled the balloon down, then the tree broke off and the balloon swooped up again, throwing one of the men out and killing him. The other four men remained in the basket and brought it down on the Laze. The five men were all French. (The 'Laze' was a grass field which belonged to the Council and was rented by farmers for grazing sheep or cattle.)

One day, I went with my uncle Jessie to Fairy's Plantation at Monks Hardwicke shooting pigeons. In the evening, leaving our bikes at The Hand in Hand public house at Toseland, we walked across the fields. My uncle managed to get there alright on his crutches, but, on the way home, the rubbers at the bottom of the crutches kept coming off and sticking in the ground. So I had to carry him, his two crutches, the two guns, the cartridges – and the pigeons! I'm not sure how many pigeons there were, but I know I picked up six with the first shot I had. It got very dark and I had that big brook to climb over. It was a long way from Monks Hardwicke to Toseland – how I did it, I shall never know!

One Saturday afternoon, Charlie Chapman from St Neots was in the Rowley's park at Monks Hardwicke, putting a few rabbit snares down, when Mr Rowley came up on his nag. He said to Charlie, "What are you up to, Charlie?" Charlie said, "I was just looking for some mushrooms, master." "Oh," said Mr Rowley, "are you sure you are not setting snares?" "No, master," said Charlie, "I don't know how to set them." Then Charlie said, "Oh, by the way, master, have you got any of your old clothes that you are finished with?" Mr Rowley replied, "No, Chapman, I haven't. Besides, my clothes wouldn't fit you." Charlie said, "Yes, they would, master. Anybody's clothes fit me." Mr Rowley was nearly as big again as Charlie!

Poor old Charlie. I remember him coming up to Mr Wagstaff, Mr Rowley's head gamekeeper, and telling him that his father was very ill and the only thing his father was asking for was rabbit. Charlie said, "Have you got one you could let him have?" Mr Wagstaff said, "Yes, I think I can find you one," which he did. The next day, Charlie came to Mr Wagstaff again, with tears running down his face and told Mr Wagstaff, "My poor old dad has gone. He passed away this morning and I haven't got anything for my dinner. Have you got another rabbit you can spare?" Mr Wagstaff said he thought he could spare another one, which he did. Charlie thanked him and left. Soon after Charlie had gone, Mr Wagstaff went down Mill Lane towards the paper mill. It was a Thursday, so he went on his way to the market in the old mule and cart. When he got to the Common gates, there was Charlie's father, opening the Common gates for people! Poor old Wagstaff often used to laugh about that.

There was an old 'doddle' tree at the bottom corner of Mr Farr's High Close, which had a hole in it. I had seen a big tawny owl come out of it a few times, so I thought it might have a nest in there. One day, I climbed up into the tree and put my hand into the hole to feel if there were any eggs. The owl was on the nest and pecked and scratched my arm and, when I pulled my hand out of the nest, it was pouring with blood.

One Saturday night, about 11 o'clock, I was on my way home, still wearing my cricketing clothes. I was under the avenue of big elm trees near the Toseland Manor. The way was dimly lit by the oil lamps on the front and back of my bike, when something hit me on the back of my head and neck. I didn't see or hear anything but I did see a bicycle light coming towards me, so I said, "You want to be careful when you are going under those trees. Someone hit me with something and made my head bleed." The cyclist turned out to be my brother Charlie, and he said, "It is an old owl and it attacked several people last night." I asked Charlie to have a look at the back of my head, so he removed his bicycle lamp and had a look. He told me my head and neck were bleeding in several places where the big owl had dug its claws in, and the blood had run down all over my white shirt and pullover. On the Monday evening, just before dark, I took my BSA air rifle up there and stood under the tree, where I thought the owl came from. In a few minutes, the owl came out of Mr Fairy's barn and flew into the tree where I stood. I put up my air rifle and hit it right under the throat and it fell down like a stone, close to my feet.

In 1923, Mr Edward Ashcroft of Graveley had some corn stacks near the top barns. They were alive with rats, so my uncle Jessie and I went and ferreted them. He stood on one side of the stacks and I stood on the other. There were two stacks and, when we had ferreted them both, we killed over 400 rats. In all my rat-catching days, I have never seen anything like it! Four ferrets were killed by the rats. One had its brain ripped open, one was bitten through the windpipe, and they all had lumps bitten out of their backs and their tails bitten off. When a ferret appeared out of a hole in the thatch, a huge rat would come out behind it and run after it up the thatch to jump on to its back. Sometimes there were two of them ripping our ferrets to pieces – and we couldn't shoot because of killing the ferrets. The terriers were kept busy as the rats bolted in all directions. The ground was covered with dead rats. Mr Ashcroft came up on his horse to see whether we were getting any rats, so I said, "Have a look around the stacks." He said, "Law-a-massey-oh! I have never seen anything like that in my life. I must say, you are doing a good job."

During the years at Friends Farm, times were very bad for farmers. Wheat was nine shillings a sack (that was 18 shillings a quarter) in 1922. We had three potato pits, each 30 yards long – and we didn't sell one potato. There was a large pit of carrots, about 26 yards long, all lovely carrots, and we didn't sell any of those either. All that work and expense for nothing. Money was very scarce in the 1920's and people just had not got the money to spend. There was a lot of unemployment. Farmers just could not afford to pay to have jobs done.

Sometimes, during hot weather, after a shower, rats would come out on the thatch and we shot them either with guns or catapults as food for the ferrets. When we were practising shooting with catapults, several of us lads would get together and stick a match on top of a gatepost, then step ten yards away – to see who could knock it off. We might also stick drawing-pins down the gatepost and then see who could drive them into the post. In the evenings, when it was dark, we filled our pockets with small potatoes, then took a torch and went round the houses to shoot the sparrows which were sitting under the eaves. Sometimes we could only see the heads of the sparrows – but that was enough. And the potatoes did not do any damage to the property.

On 26th March 1924, while living at Friends Farm, Yelling, I got married to Miss Hilda Lydia Topham, of The Hand in Hand public house, Toseland. As it was a big house, my wife and I lived in one half and the wife's mother and father lived in the other half. As well as being the landlord of the public house, the wife's father was also a small-holder and kept three horses and a pony. My wife used to ride the pony and also worked for her father. She was very handy at any farm job, especially with the horses. At that time, work was very scarce, so I would often give them a hand.

She remembered that, when she was quite a little girl, Mr Hooley called one day at The Hand in Hand and asked for a bottle of ginger beer, which cost one penny a bottle. He gave her half a crown (two shillings and sixpence) and told her to keep the change! Then he got into his carriage with the two lovely black horses and drove off.

Another memory of the Hooley Estate was from Tom Bruce, who lived at Yelling. He was working for Mr Hooley and set a snare for a hare on the way home from work one night. When he checked the snare in the morning, just before he got to it, he could see that the grass was all knocked down and muttered to himself, "Hello, old gal, you are here this morning." As he got nearer, he couldn't see the hare, so he said, "Oh, no, you're not." And the voice of the gamekeeper on the other side of the hedge said, "Oh, yes, she is," as he stood there with the hare in his hands!

When my wife was about 12 years old, during the First World War, her mother was ill in bed, so she was serving all on her own at pub. A hundred soldiers called in for a pint of beer each. An officer helped her to draw the beer and take it outside to the soldiers. They were Scots Greys from the Gun Park opposite the Priory School, St Neots, in the Rowley Estate, and they often came to the villages on exercises, sham fighting, etc. They fired blank shots from their 18-pounder in the field beside the house in which I am still living.

My wife's, father and mother were Alfred (Alf) and Lily Topham. Lily's mother (Hilda's grandmother) was a Russian Countess named

Specht, which was a German name. The countess was born in Russia and the family business was building beer vats. The family returned to Germany when the wife's mother (Lily) was 17 years old.

My wife's father often spoke about a tramp, rather a rough-looking client, who went into the taproom one evening for a drink. While he was in there, he got talking with some of the men in the pub and he said he could kill the biggest rat anyone could get, with his mouth, on his hands and knees. My wife's father said to him, "I have got some wire cages set in my buildings, so I might have a rat in one of those." The old roadster told him to go and look and, if he had got one, to bring it to the taproom and he would prove what he had said. So the wife's father fetched his lantern and went to have a look. He found a big rat in one of the cages and brought it into the taproom, which was a large room, and closed the door so it couldn't escape. Then he let the rat out of the cage and the old chap got down on his hands and knees and chased it round the room. He got it up one corner, then grabbed it with his mouth and killed it. My wife's father often talked about it.

At that time, Jim Hayden was foreman on the Croxton Estate and he asked my brother Charlie and me to help them do some threshing at Whitehall Farm, opposite The Spread Eagle. The corn he wanted to thresh was in the long shed, which was built in sections. Each bay was separate. On the Thursday before Good Friday, we had done half of the last bay, so Mr Hayden asked us if we would come in on Good Friday morning to finish it, which we did. Just before we got to the bottom, I was picking up sheaves and throwing them to my brother. He was putting them up on the drum and the sheaves were lifting up with rats. They had all worked their way along into the last bay, and there was a brick wall round three sides. We ran a piece of wire netting along the inside, so the rats could not escape – and we killed about 450 rats in that last bay.

About that time, Mr Childerley of Eltisley wanted someone to thatch a row of cottages for him, so my brother Charlie and I went to have a look at the job. On the way there, opposite Croxton Rectory, we saw two dogs burying something in a field, so I got off my cycle and went to have a look. They were burying a hare, so I picked it up and brought it across the road to show my brother. Just as I reached the road, along came the copper, P.C. Leach, who said, "I shall have to report to my superior officer that I have caught you coming off Sir Douglas Newton's land with an hare." We asked him to feel the hare, which he did, and agreed that it was not warm and had probably been killed about a week. My brother said, "You must want a job, reporting us for taking an hare that has been dead a week." But the copper did take the hare to the head gamekeeper and we were told later that he said, "If Charlie and Harold had wanted a hare, you don't think they would bother to come right over here for it, do you? I should forget all about it, if I were you."

On our way back, in the saw-mill yard opposite the school, who should we see but Sir Douglas and Lady Newton – and the manager, Mr John Fairy, known as 'Dew' Fairy. My brother and I decided that it would be best if we went and told them what had happened about the hare. As we entered the yard, Mr Fairy said, "You are just the two men we want to see." And he told us that there were several hay and clover stacks on the estate and they wondered whether we would take our hay press and press them up. We said we would do the job, piecework – and then we told them what had happened with the hare and the copper. Sir Douglas said, "Don't you worry about that, Meeks. You won't hear any more about that." And we did not.

So we did the hay pressing, which was a 'good money' job, but it was hard work. My brother did the cutting and I did the pressing. After that, we had the job of cutting a big hedge down to the ground. The hedge ran across the field opposite Barns Farm roadway towards High Hayden Farm.

In 1925, when we had finished the rabbits, my brother Charlie and I went from farm to farm doing all kinds of jobs – piecework. We did whatever job came to hand – potato digging, tree felling, thatching, sowing fertiliser (with a bucket and rope around our necks, as it was all done by hand then) and hay pressing with a hay press. We also did a lot of straw-tying, ready for thatching. Before we left in the evenings, we used to wet a large heap of straw ready for the next morning. After it had soaked all night, the straw was soft and kind to our hands and we could quickly get cracking. The price for thatching was two shillings per square, which was ten square feet. Whatever job we were doing, when we arrived in the morning, we would plot out how much we intended to do that day, then we got stuck in – and the sooner we got our whack done, the sooner we left for home!

During harvest time, when our day's work was done and we had been home for tea, we went to the allotments and cut the plots of wheat and barley for different folk. My brother did the mowing with a scythe and I tied up behind him. It was very hard work but, when you are fit and well, hard work never hurt anyone. The harder we worked, the more money we earned. Many a time we would earn more money in one day at piecework than a farm worker would earn in a week on an ordinary farm wage – but we always took pride in out work. Whatever job we did, we always made our work look nice and satisfactory. We always had good tools, which were essential, and always kept them clean and as sharp as a razor. I remember the hottest bit of stack thatching we ever did. It was almost unbearable to be on the stack – and the day after we had finished thatching it, it burst into flames and was all burnt out! Sometimes, when we were hedge trimming, we came across rose briars, which we dug up by the roots. If there were two or three briars on one root, we split the root will a bill-hook, leaving a piece of root on each briar. Each briar was about five feet long and I put fifty briars in a bundle to send by rail to various nurseries. That was all extra money on top of our week's pay. During winter months, we went brussel picking and riddling potatoes near the potato pit. I loved the brussel picking and used to say I wished there were brussels to be picked all the year round! I never wore gloves as I never suffered from cold hands. In the spring, we went into the fields, setting the brussel plants by hand.

We learned how to measure and price thatching from my father when we were children, and I have passed on this knowledge to my son Ray.

We would measure one eave, over the top and down the other eave. Suppose that measured 30 feet – then we measured the length of the stack. Suppose that also measured 30 feet. Then we multiplied the two, which made 900 feet. That would equal nine squares – a two shillings a square, that would mean we earned 18 shillings. My brother Charlie and I were thatching for a number of years, between the two wars. But there are no stacks to thatch these days.

Dry Close – 1928, opposite Yelling Chapel

From left to right Edward Reed, Frederick Peak, Walter Cullip, Joseph Mills, William Reed, Herbert Mills

Harvest on Mr Rampley's land in 1932. *From left to right* Denzil Manning of Toseland, Abey Corn of Graveley, Jack Lymage of Eltisley. Harold built the stacks, his wife Hilda is in the cart, ready to go back for another load.

YELLING CRICKET TEAM 1924

Back row Jessie Meeks (umpire), Charles Hills, Charles Harper, Sidney Currington, Walter Currington, William Reed, Thomas Leach
Front row Harold Christmas (standing, donor of the cup), Harold Meeks, Frederick Leach, Walter Meeks, Stanley Meeks, Thomas Reed, George Leach (score-keeper)

YELLING CRICKET TEAM 1929

Standing Hilda Meeks, Harold Meeks, Webb Brand, Archie Gilbert, Fred Peak, Percy Reed, Charles Meeks, Reg Meeks, Tommy Reed, Olive Leach
Sitting Vera Meeks, Ray Meeks, Buller Meeks, Charlie Harper, Stanley Meeks, Dennis Meeks, Nellie Meeks

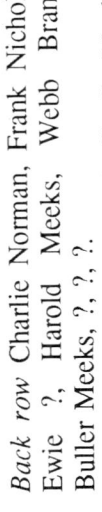

Back row Charlie Norman, Frank Nichols, Ewie ?, Harold Meeks, Webb Brand, Buller Meeks, ?, ?, ?.
Front row Charlie Catmull, Charlie Meeks, ?, Bill Giblett, Sid Elliot, ?.
There were five Meeks brothers in the team and a brother-in-law!

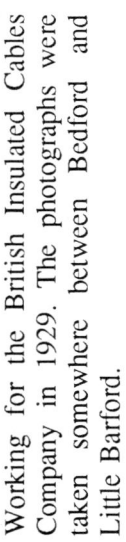

Working for the British Insulated Cables Company in 1929. The photographs were taken somewhere between Bedford and Little Barford.

One day, Tom Barnes, who owned a greengrocer's shop in St Neots market square, asked me to plant a two-acre plot of brussels for him. I did so, on my own, in one day – 9680 plants! Not a bad day's work! When they had been planted about two weeks, Mr Barnes pulled a few plants for 'filling up' the crop but, although he walked all over the two-acre plot, he didn't set a single plant – there were no gaps! He made a special journey to my house to congratulate me on my marvellous piece of work. In most areas, years ago, farmers grew a field of brussels to find work for piecework gangs and, about half past two or three o'clock, the men could be seen carrying the bags of brussels from the fields on to the roadside ready to be picked up by the lorries for the markets. Some went to London and some to the North. But all that has died out now – the crops are just corn and rape.

I also planted two acres of potatoes for my father in the Gorse Allotment in one day and every potato was **put** in place, not thrown in as some folk used to do. Mr Barnes asked me if I would take my scythe to Southoe to mow an acre of barley for him. I did so, one Saturday, and, as I passed Southoe Church, the clock struck eight o'clock. I went towards Midlow to the allotment and there I fitted my scythe and got cracking. I mowed the acre of barley, tied it up, set it up in stooks and hand-dragged the whole plot. I tied up the draggings, tied up my scythe and gathering rake on my cycle and made for home. When I passed Southoe Church on my way back home, the clock struck four o'clock – and I thought to myself, "That is a good day's work!"

There was no work about so, one day just before harvest, six of us from Yelling cycled to Whittlesey, through Thorney and out to Guyhirn, then round to Somersham and St Ives and back to Yelling – and we could not get a job anywhere. There were lots of haystacks in the Fen, but each farmer said he could not afford to have them thatched. So there was no work – even after cycling over 100 miles.

Then I heard that a Shredded Wheat factory was going to be built at Welwyn, so I cycled there and was standing on the site when two men came along with a measuring tape and knocked the first peg into the ground. I asked whether there was any chance of a job and they told me to come back in two weeks' time, when there might be a chance of employment. But, when I cycled there in two weeks' time, I found about 100 men waiting for a job. I found lodgings and stayed there for a week – but no luck. Then I tried for a job on the Letchworth Garden City sewer, so I was there each day but, although I stayed there for a week, there was still no luck as there were hundreds of men waiting for a job. So I came home.

Eventually Papworth Colony (Papworth Village Settlement) wanted my two brothers (and me) to lay a cricket pitch for them, near the church at Papworth Everard, which we did. I played on it many times and it 'played very nicely'. After a while, it was built on and they asked us if we would lay another – near the poultry farm on Mr Hayman's grass field, which was 'high-backed' land and the hollows were full of water. The pitch was to be 50 yards square, so we lifted up all the turf, then dug off all the hills level with the hollows, then drained it and then put back the turf which was in good condition. When it was made into playing order, the players said their pitch was 'second to none'. It was said that it was a perfect pitch and 'played lovely'.

My son Raymond (Ray) was born on 6th April 1927. About nine o'clock in the evening, the midwife said to me, "Harold, you'd better get on your bike and go to Caxton to get Dr Dudley." I did so and Dr Dudley came and said that the baby would not be born before morning, so I would have to fetch him again. At two o'clock next morning, Mrs Revell (the midwife) said, "I'm afraid you will have to go to Caxton again, Harold." It was pouring with rain and I was soaked to the skin long before I got to Caxton. On my first journey, I had been stopped by the Police because of fowl-stealers, so I was expecting to be stopped again. When I got halfway between Eltisley and Caxton Gibbet, a light flashed in front of me and someone said, "Stop!" – it was another copper. I said, "It's Meeks from Toseland. Don't make me get off my bike, as water is running down my body." So they told me to carry on. Then, when I got to the Gibbet, two lights flashed in front of me and I said, "It's Meeks again, Sergeant." The sergeant knew me quite well, having played cricket with me, so he said, "OK, carry on." When I got to the doctor's, he said, "You had better leave your cycle here and ride back with me," which I did. Then I came back with him, when it was all over. Ray was born at seven o'clock in the morning and Dr Dudley had breakfast with us. He had eggs and bacon – and whiskey in his tea! He told us it was the best breakfast he had had in his life!

About this time, we heard that the British Insulated Cables Company were going to put up poles and electric cables in this area, so, one morning, Charlie and I cycled to the other side of Eynesbury, where they had just started putting a wooden pole line up. The foreman said, "Go to Sandy and see the general foreman – they are just going to start on a steel tower line." So we cycled to the dump at Sandy and found about 60 men waiting for a job. The head one picked out about ten from the 60 – and my brother and I were among the ten, I dug the first hole in that line. When the foreman came along, just before we had finished digging, he said to me, "That's not the first hole you have dug, eh?" But I said it was! He said he had been on the job for a long time and it was the best hole he had seen dug. From the on, he would often fetch me to put the holes in shape that other men had dug. We carried on from Sandy to Little Barford – then on to Godmanchester.

When my brother Charlie and I started working for the British Insulated Cables Company, the foreman was so pleased with our work that he said, "Have you got any more brothers who would like a job?" so we told him that we had two more brothers – Buller and Stanley. The foreman said, "Bring them along then." So they started work about two or three days after us.

When we were on the Port Holme at Godmanchester, we were marking the holes out in ice and we had three or four pumps working on each hole. The day before Christmas, we had got all the holes dug (seven in number), and a steel tower erected in each hole, with four ropes on each tower fastened to crowbars in the ground – all ready for concreting after dinner. While we were sitting on a heap of timber eating our dinner, someone out on the Port Holme said, "Look at the river. It is overflowing!" And it was! The water was coming in at a fast rate, so we packed up our food and began to build the timber up higher. In a few minutes, we were surrounded by water, which kept on rising until it was four feet deep or more, and we wondered what was going to happen next. Then two of Jack Barringer's men, Tom Clifton and Cherry Merry, came to fetch us off with two horses and a trolley. The men sat on the backs of the horses, with their feet up on the chains, to keep them out of the water. As we left, we saw all our timber go sailing down the river. When we went back after Christmas, everything had gone – the timber, the pikes we had for raising the towers, several bags of coke, earth-plates, sand and gravel, spades, shovels, picks – everything! The seven steel towers, that were fastened down with ropes and crowbars, had all floated across the Port Holme and into the river. The tops of the poles with the insulators attached were sticking in the bottom of the river and the bottoms of the poles were sticking up into the air! So we fetched three horses, pulled the poles out and started all over again. As the poles had made their way across Port Holme towards the river, the insulators had cut out deep furrows all the way – just as if it had been done with a plough.

When that line was finished, we helped to put up a wooden pole line from Godmanchester to St Ives and from St Ives to Histon. When we reached the other side of Swavesey, the weather was very hot and we slept under a big sheet in the fields. One night, before I got into bed, I noticed a rabbit's run close to my bed, so I set a rabbit snare in the run. When I woke in the morning, the rabbit was laying beside me, in the snare. I said to my mates, "Look here! This is the first time I have laid in bed and taken a rabbit out of a snare!"

When we finished that line, we ran a line from Potters Bar to Wealdstone and found lodgings in Potters Bar. One Sunday morning, we left our lodgings and my brother Buller, my step-brother Webb and I went to see where a Zeppelin had crashed during the First World War. It crashed on a big oak tree, close to the trunk, but the other side of the tree was untouched. We collected a lot of remains of the Zeppelin. That one was brought down by anti-aircraft fire. The Zeppelin that came down at Cuffly was brought down by a Lieutenant Robinson's aircraft. We also visited the graveyard and saw the graves of the two crews. There were 35 dead altogether, 19 in one Zeppelin and 16 in the other. On each of the iron slabs was inscribed a record of the name, rank and number of each dead German.

While we were working at Potters Bar, one of the bosses asked my brother Buller and me if we would go to Elstree, where he was living, near the film studios, to concrete a garage floor for him. While I was doing that job, I had the pleasure of opening the garden gate for Anna-May Wong, the actress, who was living in the bungalow next door. She was wearing a lovely silver-grey fox fur coat. At that moment, Douglas Fairbanks Senior walked past, close to where I was opening the gate.

He had just left the studio and was wearing uniform — a red tunic with yellow braids, striped trousers and a sword in its sheath. It seemed to be quite an honour to be so close to them.

When that job was finished, we went on a big grid line job from Clapham, near Bedford, to Little Barford. While we were on that job, I was promoted to 'leading hand,' which was written on my pay packet each week. That gave me responsibility for setting the tables for boring the holes for each leg of those big towers. This was very tricky, as every hole had to be measured exactly, otherwise the tower would not stand upright. For that work, I received an extra tuppence an hour. When the holes were bored — some nine feet deep and some 12 feet — it was my job to blow a hole two feet in diameter at the bottom of every hole. This was done with gelignite and I had to use my own judgment as to how much gelignite to use. The soil that came out of the hole was the only clue I had to go by — and the soil varied from site to site. When each hole had been blown out, I had calipers down the hole and, as I pulled the handle up, the bottom opened and the numbers at the top would tell me the size of the hole at the base. If it was two feet — that was OK!

When we got near the river at Little Barford end, the holes all had to be dug because it was all clear gravel and, as the holes were well below the river level, no boring could be done. I got another extra tuppence and hour for that, for working in water. I had to get down into the holes, which had to be lined with timber all round to keep the sides up. When I was scraping the gravel from the sides of the holes, which were eight feet square, there were men up at the top (at ground level) driving the planks down until we were deep enough to keep the water out, so I could work comfortably. We had seven hand pumps, with two men on each pump, and a motor pump with a ten-inch outlet. But if one pump stopped for a minute, I had to scramble out of the hole as quickly as possible since the water rose very quickly.

On our way home from Renhold, after a working day, my brother-in-law, Arthur Currington and I were riding on a motorbike and sidecar. He was on the motorbike and I was in the sidecar, when we hit a ten-ton lorry (a Horniman's Tea lorry) head on. My brother-in-law was killed instantly. It happened outside the *Bell* public house between Wyboston and Eaton Socon.

Plans had already been made for both of us to travel with the firm to Scotland to do the same kind of work but, because of the accident, the plans were all broken. I turned the job down, as I did not want to go to Scotland on my own. I did have a motorbike of my own, but I covered it up with a sheet and didn't even look at it for six months or so after the accident. I pedalled my way from Toseland to Clapham and all parts of the line where we were working, leaving home in the dark in the mornings to get to work at Clapham for eight o'clock.

I left Clapham in the dark at night with two oil lamps on my bike. If it was windy, the lamps kept going out, or caught fire. Some mornings, when I left home, it was pouring with rain or there was a strong wind – and it always seemed to be a head wind all the way to work! Then, after work with a pick-axe all day and then cycling 17 miles to and from work, I was often so tired that, when I got home, I flopped down in the armchair and my wife washed me. Then I had my tea and didn't move again until I went to bed. In the morning, it was the same old thing again.

Those were what we called the good old days! But the wages paid on those jobs were better than on the farm. The next job was to run another line from Little Barford to Cambridge. That was a beam pole line. We had to climb the poles on 'skates'. The skates were very like those worn on ice. We fastened them to our boots then, to climb the pole, we placed one foot on each side of the steel pole. On the skates were a bullet and a diamond and, to climb the pole, we lifted our heel for each step upward then we dropped our heel and the skate would grip to the pole. Then we did the other foot the same – then kept doing so until we reached the top. When the line was erected, four of us painted the poles. My step-brother, Webb Brand, and I painted from the top as far down as the barbed-wire guards and the other two men painted from there to the bottom. We finished each pole by fitting the barbed-wire guards and 'Danger' plates.

We then painted the first line we had erected – from Sandy to Little Barford – and then from Little Barford to Godmanchester. Horace Human and I painted from the top to the barbed-wire guards and Mac Smith and Herbert Barringer did the rest to the bottom. Then we ended our work with the British Insulated Cables Company.

I then went to work for the Bedfordshire, Cambridgeshire and Huntingdonshire Electricity Board (B.C & H for short), helping to put up low tension lines in towns and villages. My main job was cutting branches off trees which were in the way of the line where the wires were coming. The work was sometimes very awkward when the branches were overhanging the houses in the streets. We had to be careful not to damage property. One day, we were putting poles up in Needingworth and I was digging a hole in someone's garden for a stay-block. The stay-block was a large block of wood, which was buried six feet under the ground. Then a stay-rod, which was a steel cable, was fixed on the top of an electric tower and then on to the stay-block in order to keep the tower upright where there was an angle in the electric line. I had just put the block in place under the house, six feet deep, and was just standing upright on the stay-block, when the earth all around me closed in – and buried me up to my neck! The chap who was digging the hole for the pole heard me grunt when the earth closed in and he came running into the garden – and could only see my head! He quickly fetched the foreman, Molly Chalky, and he got two more men to dig me out, but I couldn't move until they had cleared the earth away almost to my feet. If it had happened just a minute sooner, when I was pushing the block under the house, I would have been completely buried. It was a frightening experience.

When we were putting a line up from Kate's Cabin to Wansford, in almost every hole we found Roman pottery. A man from a museum came every day and collected the pieces. He gave us a few shillings for a drink for keeping them for him. When digging the holes, we were digging in layers of iron-stone – no soil at all. The stones were all flat – a lot of them as big as dinner plates. Very different from digging at Gogmagog Hills near Cambridge, where, after we dug off about three inches of turf, it was all pure white chalk – whiter than snow.

We also dug some holes at Alwalton, near Peterborough, and, when we got to 18 inches deep, we came to a layer of rock and there was no way we could pierce it. At Clapham, near Bedford, that same layer of rock was seven feet below the surface.

When I was working for the B.C & H Electricity Company, instead of going home for my tea, I went to tea with Mr Boswell in Avenue Road or with Mr and Mrs Pibworth in Cambridge Street. I helped each evening to cart their corn with Mr Wager's big lorry. Two or three men pitched the sheaves up on the lorry, while I loaded them. When they were loaded, we took Mr Boswell's corn up to the Shortsands Yard, where I did the stacking. One evening, in order to finish a field, I put a great big high load on the lorry. When we got to the railway bridge, we couldn't get under it. So Mr Wager turned his lorry round and went back along the Cambridge road as far as The Spread Eagle, Croxton, then down the road through Toseland village and all the way round, through St Neots, to get that great big load to Shortsands. While we were unloading, it dropped in dark and I had to put the roof on the stack by the light of the lamps of another lorry. When I had finished the stack, we had quite a lot of corn left over, so Mr Boswell asked me to build another smaller stack, which I did. It was 11 pm when I started to build the smaller stack and we could see the lightning in the distance and hear the thunder and we were afraid it would reach us before we were finished. But I had just finished when it started to rain. Mr Wager took me home, carrying my cycle in his lorry – and that was between 12 o'clock and one o'clock in the morning. We couldn't have finished the job without the lorries to provide the light.

I also did the same for Mr Pibworth and did his thatching. Also, in my spare time, I did the stacking for Dick Maddy of Cambridge Street and his brother George of Eynesbury – and also for Mr Billy Harvey.

I went to the Wembley Exhibition in 1926, when we saw the first combines, and people said they would never be able to use them in this county – but that turned out to be wrong. We also saw milking machines. But what I was most interested in was watching them making Cream Crackers and caramel toffees. To make Cream Crackers, they had what was just like a track off a crawler tractor, which was going round and round. The track was in sections and was very hot. A girl was sitting at the end of the track and, as the sections came round, we could see the liquid running on to the sections. By the time each section got to the girl, the crackers were baked, and the girl took a square of crackers (100 in each square) off the track and stacked them in a heap beside her. It was very interesting. And so was the making of the caramels. We could see the liquid running on to a hot plate, then the caramels came out along an elevator, all wrapped in their papers ready for sale in thousands. I spent a lot of time watching them.

In 1930, we moved from Wayside to Lodge Farm along the Toseland road, where we lived for three and a half years. One day, I was planting brussel plants. Just as my steel dibb was going into the ground, a flash of lightning played around – all pretty colours – and the ground turned grey all round the dibb, where it had been burnt. I went so dizzy I could hardly stand up, so I waited for a while, then I walked up the field to old Ted Revell, who was hoeing. He said, "You look funny." I said, "I've been struck by lightning." He told me to go home and, when I arrived there and walked inside, my wife said, "Whatever is the matter?" I explained what had happened and she also told me I looked funny, so I went and looked in the mirror. I rubbed my finger down my face and found it was covered with soot. Next day, I could peel the skin off my face. No doubt it was that steel dibb that saved my life.

Sixty years ago, when spring drilling was on the go, I often went to the field of drilling before daybreak, ready for the pigeons to come out. Many a time I have had anything from 50 to 100 pigeons, taken them home and got to work at seven o'clock. I only wish I could do it now!

One day, as I was shooting pigeons on Mr Farley's field, not far from Toseland Wood, I saw several go into the wood. I knew they would be dead birds when they got into the woods, so I went into the wood to pick them up. While I was in the wood, a pigeon flew over me, so I shot it down. It lodged on a Haw-bush, so I shook it down and, as I grabbed hold of the pigeon, a fox tried to get it out of my hand. I put the pigeon behind my back and kicked the fox. It went about ten yards from me, stopped, turned and started to come back towards me. I thought it might attack me, so I gave it the other barrel – and that was that!

By the way, a Haw-bush is a whitethorn bush, which produces the white flowers called 'May'. When the flowers die, the fruit forms, which is called 'Haw'. At first, it is green in colour, later it turns red and provides food for the birds during the winter.

In 1929, the St Neots cinema caught fire. I also remember seeing Eaton Socon church on fire when I was on my way home one Saturday night in 1930.

I bought my first 12-bore gun from old Jimmy Tack for three shillings. It was a bolt-action gun and, the first time I took it out, I went on Mr Joe Thoday's field of clover, not far from Cotton's Farm. It was alive with pigeons, so I got in a big hedge and waited until they got within shooting distance, then I fired and I waited to see if I could get another shot. As I waited, I could see that some of the pigeons I had shot were struggling away, so I went to pick the others up. I picked about 12 up but, if I had gone out sooner, I could have picked up about 18. I thought that was not bad with the first shot with the old gun.

On another occasion, I was standing in my hide in a big hedge between Mr Harley's and Mr Warboy's land, when there was such a clatter and a sparrow-hawk dived into the hide after a sparrow – and caught it about nine inches from my face. I put up my hand and took the sparrow out of the sparrow-hawk's claws. The hawk remained still, close to my face for several minutes, then flew up and over my head and hovered there for a few minutes – then flew away. In about 20 minutes, the hawk came back to the very same spot and hovered just above my head for about five minutes. Some folks say that sparrow-hawks don't hover – but I can assure you that they do!

For a number of years, work was very scarce and there was a very long dole queue at St Neots, reaching a long way down New Street. My brother Charlie and I could have stayed on the dole for a long time, as we had a lot of stamps on our stamp cards. At that time, there were two kinds of stamps – tradesmen's stamps and agricultural stamps. Through working for the Electricity Board for such a long time, we had tradesmen's stamps and we earned one pound, six shillings and ninepence a week. We took on the job of trimmming all the hedges on Papworth and Papley Grove Farms for Mr Pamplin – at one pound, nine shillings and threepence – so we received two shillings and sixpence a week more for working all week than we were getting on the dole for doing nothing! When we finished the hedge trimming job, we were out of work again and went back to sign on the dole. They told us we could not sign back on the dole again as we had lost all our stamps because we had been working on the land for six months! If we hadn't gone to work on the land, we could have stayed on the dole indefinitely! If ever there was a funny law, that was one!

Those who didn't want a job or wouldn't take one if they had the chance were still on the dole, but we, who wanted to work, could not get any dole money.

The only job that came along was pea-picking. As soon as there was a field of peas ready for picking, there were men, women and children – perhaps 100 or more in the field. When a bag had been filled, it was carried to the weighing machine, where it was weighed and the man in charge would either give the picker a token, or he would record each bag in a book. When the field was finished, the picker would receive his, or her, money. The best time to pick was in the morning, when the dew was on the peas. They weighed more and handled much better. Many a time I have been sitting in a field at three o'clock in the morning, waiting for it to get light, so I could see to start picking. At times, when each picker was rationed to a certain number of bags, I have had my number picked and I've been on my way home when the others were just coming to make a start on theirs.

Mr John Chapman (Jack), son of Mr Thomas Chapman of Monks Hardwicke, where they farmed, asked me if I would sow a field of soot for him – and I agreed. The best time to do that job was at night, when the dew was falling. The field was near the farm and the bags of soot were already out in the field. To get to the field, I had to cross the brook, in which there was quite a lot of warm water, so I went in daylight to pick a shallow place to cross over. It would be dark when I returned to sow the soot, so I choose a certain tree for a marker. At two o'clock in the morning I set off to start the job. It was pitch dark and, when I got to the brook, I chose the wrong tree for a marker and the bank was very steep – and I slipped down the bank and into deep water. I got soaked and, when I reached the field, it was so dark I couldn't see the bags of soot, so I had to sit and wait for daylight to come. I was soaking wet, cold and uncomfortable.

While I was working at Monks Hardwicke, Mr Jack Chapman told me that Mr Miles, the timber merchant's men had felled 100 trees on Monks Hardwicke Farm and asked whether I would like the job of clearing all the branches up and burning them. I took on the job at ten shillings per top. There was a lot of wood in some of the tops and, if the tree trunk split when the tree fell, the men cut through the tree below the split – so I had part of the trunk to burn as well. Where there were big trunks which I could not move, that was where I lit my fire, packing the other smaller bits of wood all around it.

Then Mr Jack Chapman asked me if I would mow round and tie all his fields on Monks Hardwicke Farm, ready for the binder, which I did for two shillings an acre. Altogether, there were about 700 acres. When the corn was cut, stooked and ready for carting, Mr Jack Chapman offered me the contract of carting the corn from all the fields, with me doing the pitching on to the carts and my son, Ray, who was on holiday from school, doing the loading. I said I would do the job if he promised I would never have to wait for the carts. He said he would see to it that I had plenty of carts – which he did. He had a spare waggon standing in the field all the time.

One night, when we had finished loading and went up to the stack, Mr Jack Chapman said to me, "Well, Harold, that is the most corn I have carted away in one day in my life." He laughed and said, "Harvest won't last long at this rate." When harvest was finished, I took on the job of thatching all the stacks.

Then my brother Charlie and I went digging potatoes on the Croxton Estate, for which we were paid ten shillings a ton – for digging and picking up. When we were finished that, Mr 'Dew' Fairy, the manager, asked if we would cut down all the dead trees on the Croxton Estate. That was a full winter's work, up to the end of March. From that job, we went on planting potatoes, then we did some hoeing on the Fruit Farm, up to haytime, when we went from farm to farm thatching the stacks – all at piecework rates.

Then, while we were thatching some haystacks for Messrs Pamplin Brothers at Papley Grove, the manager, Mr Howe, said they had two fields of tares which were flat to the ground and couldn't be cut with the grass-cutters, so he asked us to swob them, and help with the harvest. It was jolly hard work, swobbing tares, as they were very long and tangled, but swobbing did a nice clean job (when it was done properly), and no seed was lost. There is a picture of me with a swob on the back cover.

The swob was only used for cutting peas or tares. When swobbing, I had a straight stick with a fork tine fixed at the bottom for lifting the peas off the ground. I carried this hook in my left hand and then the swob in my right hand. I put my hand through the leather loop at the top of the handle and reached down to the hand grip halfway down the swob stick. The leather loop where I put my arm through was to help control my cutting, otherwise the cutting blade would go anywhere, and I would soon be cutting my own legs! The blade was very sharp. It was a scythe blade cut short – to about 18 inches in length. When the swob was used properly, it cut the tares or peas off cleanly at their base and did not hit or disturb the seed. This was a dangerous job and needed great concentration in order not to hit anything other than the crop.

After that job, we helped with the harvest. My brother and I went into the fields and loaded the carts. There were six of us in the gang. One day, we were all stooking in a field of beans near Yelling Wood, using two-tine forks, because there were a lot of thistles in the beans. There were two gypsy chaps with us in the gang and they started quarrelling. One of them ran at the other with his fork as if to stick him with it. As he went past, my brother Charlie grabbed hold of him, put him to the ground and took the fork away from him. Charlie said to him, "We don't allow that sort of thing here, so bear that in mind!"

The other gypsy told us how many minutes the First World War lasted. He explained it all to us, including one leap year, and he wrote it all down on paper and it was two and a quarter million minutes. He also said, "You can ask me any question you like about the Bible and I will answer it." So we asked him a few questions (ones we knew the answers to!) and he answered no trouble. After tea one evening, I got our family Bible and wrote down several questions, noting down the chapter and the verse. I took the paper with me next morning and, at lunchtime, I asked the gypsy the questions – but I hadn't got one he couldn't answer, and that surprised us all.

When we finished harvest, my brother Charlie and I did all the thatching for two shillings a square. After that, we took out a hay presser for Messrs Innes and Co. of Stevenage. As they bought the stacks, we pressed them into half-hundredweight trusses. After a while, I left my brother to make room for his son, Dennis, who took my place with his father for a long time. (Today, Dennis has his own building business in St Neots.)

When my wife and I were at the pictures one Saturday evening, they showed us pictures of the Prime Minister, Neville Chamberlain, getting off a plane after seeing Hitler. He was waving a piece of paper saying 'peace in our time' – which didn't stand for much!

Then I contracted to do the harvest for Mr Ramply, who at that time farmed along the Toseland road. The contract was to mow round ready for the binder at two shillings an acre and, when it was cut, to set it up for four shillings an acre. When it stood in stooks for two weekends, it was ready for carting and putting into stacks. For that job, I received six shillings an acre. Then I did all the thatching. I was very fond of thatching, which I did single-handed, without a partner, for two shillings a square. I had just contracted to do the harvest, when the Second World War broke out. We were told to take our gas masks with us where ever we went.

Poor old Abey Corn had been to Yelling Feast and was on his way home, up the old bridle road, very much the worse for drink. It was a pitch dark night and he said he met the Devil, who had a three-tined fork and chains around his neck. The Devil stood in front of him and said, "Corn, if you touch a drop more beer, I will stick this fork through you." Abey said, "He frightened the life out of me!" Poor old Abey, we used to get a laugh out of him. He was helping with the harvest when the Second World War started. On the Sunday evening, the Prime Minister spoke and advised everyone to take their gas-masks with them. When we got to work, we were going a long way down the fields, so we all had our gas-masks with us – except Abey! I said to him, "Aren't you bringing your gas-mask, Abey?" He said, "No. I'm not taking no gas-mask and more wouldn't you if you had been in the First World War." So we went quite a long way down the fields and we hadn't been there long when the siren went. Poor old Abey – he ran back to the buildings for his gas-mask and we kept pulling his leg about it. He would get so awkward because Jack Lymage would keep on saying "Acorn, Acorn".

Just before the Second World War, we had some relations down from London on holiday. We used to walk down to Great Paxton for a drink and, on our way home, we used to sing the old songs. One I remember especially:

When you go down the Lambeth way,
Any evening, any day,
You will find them all
Doing the Lambeth walk.

We were all enjoying ourselves and watching the searchlights that were dotted about in the villages, shining up into the sky – a pretty sight. It was not long after that when we heard Neville Chamberlain give out on the wireless that we were at war with Germany – September 1939.

It wasn't long after that we heard that they were going to build another aerodrome quite close to us, at Graveley. They soon began to clear all the trees and hedgerows, making a real clearance. They also cut down all the trees in Toseland Wood, as the number three runway was in line with the wood – and also in line with Toseland Manor House, so they fixed a big red light on the top of one of the chimneys. The Toseland road is a very historic road because, in Roman times, there was a large castle in the middle of the wood, surrounded by a large moat, which is still there. When the aerodrome was finished, there were three runways. The main one ran from Graveley to Great Paxton, number two ran from the Graveley corner, in line with Offord, and number three, which I have already written about, ran from Graveley to Offord Road and over Toseland Wood. The first planes to come to Graveley were Whitley twin-engine bombers and Lysanders, but they soon left and arrangements were made for me to take a dart team to the Corporal's Dining Hall on Saturday evening, 14th March 1943. Then on the evening before that, Squadron Leader Moody came to see me and he said, "Don't bring your dart team tomorrow evening, Harold. The thirty-fifth T.L. Squadron of Halifax bombers [the Pathfinders] are coming in at one o'clock on Saturday."

As we had just left our work on the Saturday and were coming up the track from the camp, the whole squadron came very low, just over our heads, and landed on number three runway. Then, each day, when we came home from work, we could see them all standing on their dispersal points, glistening in the sunshine, some quite close to the road. It was a lovely sight. Then things started to liven up in all the pubs in the villages and we got to know a lot of airmen and the aircrews. We played darts quite a bit with them. On several occasions, we had a very enjoyable evening with them, then they would say to me, "We shan't see you tomorrow night, pal, as we are going on 'ops' – but we will still see you the next night." But on that next night, I watched and waited for them, but they didn't turn up. Then some of their mates would turn up and tell me the sad news, that they had been shot down. Most evenings, just before dusk, we could see the aircrews going to their planes, which were standing on their dispersal points, all loaded up with bombs ready for take-off. Some were loaded so heavy, they couldn't rise and would crash on take-off. It was a wonderful sight, to see the planes come to life, with each engine starting up in turn and the flames leaping from their exhausts. Then the planes would taxi round the perimeter track and on to the runway, in turn, ready for take-off. They would wait at the end of the runway for the green light in the control tower to flash for them to take off. A few of the planes would have engine failure and would have to unload their bombs to stop it from crashing. As the airfields were only a few miles apart and the bombers were all taking off from each airfield at the same time, they would keep circling round and round until they all got airborne, then off they would go in their hundreds, with the sky looking full of planes. Then the runway lights went out and all was quiet until the early hours of the morning, when we used to get woken up by the planes returning.

Often we would open our bedroom windows and watch the runway lights come on. We saw the planes coming in to land. Some were shot up very badly and could only crashland. We could see the ambulances and fire engines waiting for them to land and the groundcrews waiting for their planes to return, but I am sorry to say that some of them waited in vain. There were times when Jerry was waiting for the runway lights to come on and would follow our planes in. But if Jerry was in the area, our lot would switch off the runway lights and wouldn't give our airmen permission to land.

Later in the war, the aircraft changed from Halifaxes to Lancasters and Mosquitoes. There was also F.I.D.O. (FIDO), which was the only system in the country at that time for dispersing fog. It was laid on each side to the main runway, which was the one running from Graveley to Great Paxton, and it consisted of three large pipes on each side of the runway and stretching to its full length. Each pipe was full of small holes. When the petrol was pumped along it squirted through the holes and, when it was set alight, it was a wonderful sight. We didn't need any lights in our house when it was on! It had to take all the planes from other airfields when it was foggy. As there were so many of them, it took a long time for them to land. Sometimes the planes would be flying around so long, waiting for their turn to land, that they would run out of fuel and crash. One morning, when there was very thick fog, we were on our way to work, when we saw a number of planes which had crashed – most of them all burnt out. One plane crashed on the stacks of bombs in the bomb dump and some landed on the grass, in bushes, anywhere on the airfield, or anywhere around it. When FIDO was alight, we could hear the roar a long way off and see clouds of black smoke going up into the sky, lifting the fog as it rose. FIDO used thousands of gallons of petrol every minute. The first time it was used, people came from miles around when they saw the sky all lit up.

In May 1940, I was visiting my brother Arthur and his wife at Yelling, when Sir Anthony Eden made his appeal for volunteers for the L.D.V. (Local Defence Volunteers), later called the Home Guard. The next evening, when I arrived home from work and had had my tea, I got on my bike and went down to St Neots Police Station. When I knocked at the door of the police station, the policeman, who was in the office, said, "Come in", which I did.

He asked, "What can I do for you?" I told him I had come to volunteer for the LDV. He said, "You are the second one to join. There has been one before you." This was Mr Hawarth from Yelling, who became captain of the Toseland and Yelling platoon. Then the policeman took my name, address, height and shoe size – and when I arrived home from work the next evening, as I walked in the house, the first thing I saw was my uniform laying on the settee and my boots beside it and my rifle standing in the corner, with five rounds of ammunition. There was a note asking me to go round to the village recruiting so, when I had finished my tea, I put on my uniform and went round to Yelling and picked up 13 recruits, which I took to Captain Hawarth. He said, "Well done. That is a good start!"

In 1941, an aeroplane crashed in Barnfield Lane, near Papworth St Agnes. We were working up the hill at the time of the crash, halfway up between Barnfield Lane and Dumptilow Farm, when we saw the Sterling bomber, which I think had just taken off from Wyton Airfield. We heard an explosion and saw flames coming out from one of the engines. We watched it change course towards Graveley but, as it came near Barnfield Lane, it crashed into some tall trees – then there was a terrible explosion. It had just filled up with fuel. When we heard and saw the explosion, we ran to the stack of bean-straw, where we had left our cycles. We thought thay might get burnt, so the first thing we did was to move them away to a safer place. Then we quickly went to the place of the crash. The first thing we saw was a Gypsy man grazing his horse on the roadside, a few yards from the crash. Then we saw one of the airmen lying beside him, with his head split open, right across his forehead. He was quite dead. Then I saw the rear gunner running across Mr Sperling's grass field, and he was all in flames. I ran across the field and threw my arms around his neck to put the flames out, but the poor man's face and hands were just bubbling, like a joint of meat which had been in the oven for some time. Then I saw the huge landing wheel, which was running along in front of the crashed plane, it passed by the Gypsy – and went straight for Harry Billing's men, who were putting up potatoes. Then it ran up a sloping bank, which caused it to roll over, otherwise it could have caused serious trouble to the farm workers. The field where the men were working was on Baldock Farm (Cottage Farm).

One night, my son Ray and I were standing outside our house. We saw a Stirling bomber, which had just taken off from Wyton Airfield and was flying quite low with its lights on. It was not far from our house, when two German fighter-planes came diving down. One of them gave the Stirling a burst of machine-gun fire, then turned away. In came the other plane and gave the Stirling another burst of fire. We saw an airman bale out and his parachute landed in the middle of a hedge at the back of the reservoir at Toseland Road. Soon afterwards, some airmen from Graveley Airfield came to our house to ask us if we had seen anything and we told them where the airman had landed. They asked us if we had seen more than one man bale out – but we had not. We heard afterwards that one airman did bale out, up at Hill Farm, Papworth St Agnes. All the others were killed as the plane crashed on the A14 road, near the brook about 500 yards from Kisby's Hut.

One Saturday evening, a Mosquito plane crashed into the big elm trees near the Toseland Manor House and burnt out, killing the two airmen. There was another crash, close to that one, on another occasion, when a Halifax bomber returning from a raid on Germany crashed on the wayside buildings and demolishing the lot – corn barn, stable, cart shed and henhouses. It narrowly missed the house where my wife and my son Ray were born and where my wife's parents lived for 30 years. The plane landed in the garden, in a small pond where my wife's father used to dip out the water for his horse. Only the rear-gunner escaped alive – all the rest were drowned.

A team of us locals played the Air Force on Graveley Airfield one Sunday afternoon in, I think, 1944. While we were playing, my son Ray was batting and the M.O. was bowling. He was one of the West Indies cricketers. As he was running up to bowl, some of the airmen were fusing the bombs in the fusing shed. One of the bombs exploded, killing seven airmen in the shed and a piece of the bomb, about ten inches long, fell against my son's feet. That spoilt our game. We were going mowing around the wheat-field close to the bomb dump on the following Monday morning, ready for the tractor and binder to come and cut the wheat, but on the Sunday evening, Squadron Leader Moody came to see me and told me not to work there for a week, in case there were any more explosions.

When the airfield closed down, the farmer who was going to farm it asked me if I would take the job to clear all the bushes and rubbish, so that he could get the land ready for cropping. One day I asked the farmer, "What are all these cars doing, coming on the 'drome'?" He said, "Don't you know?" I told him I didn't. He said, "Those big feeding pipes that fed FIDO are full of petrol, thousands of gallons, and there are several taps, where they can go and help themselves. Havn't you got any out of it?" And I said, "No, I haven't." The farmer said, "Go and help yourself, just whenever you like. I have been using it for some time now. When they take FIDO away, all the petrol that is left in the pipes will be wasted."

Now the whole airfield is being farmed by Mr Martin Eayrs and Mr Marvin Thoday. Mr Martin Eayrs is the son of Mr Robert Eayrs, who farmed most of the airfield before the war. He also farmed at Leighton Bromswold, where he lived. Others who farmed parts of the airfield before the war were Mr Currington of Graveley, Mr W Fairy of Toseland and Mr Richard (Dick) Setchell of Graveley. Now those great wide runways have all been fetched up, leaving a narrow track for the tractors and farm implements, or cars, etc., to use. The control tower has been made into the farmhouse. Whenever we take a ride round the old airfield, it certainly brings back a lot of memories.

Our Home Guard H.Q. was in Toseland Reading Room, where we had two beds. Our N.C.O.s were regular soldiers in the First World War. Our commanding officer, Captain Hawarth, had been a major in the First World War. Although Toseland and Yelling had two separate platoons, Captain Hawarth was the commanding officer of them both. On several occasions, the two platoons amalgamated.

The Toseland platoon consisted of 22 members and each night we did two shifts of four hours each. The first shift was from 8pm to midnight and the second shift from midnight to 4am. We always worked in pairs, two for each shift. For a long period, our regular route was as follows: from my house, along the Toseland road, through Toseland village, then through Yelling village and up to the Eltisley – St Ives road, then past the Papley Grove cottages and up to the searchlight camp, where we had to sign our names in a book, so that our captain would know we had done our job.

After a while, things changed and we had to go the other way towards the railway. We had to inspect all the railway bridges in our area to see if there were any bombs or other items planted under the bridges. When we had done our four hours' duty, especially during harvest-time, when our day's work was so long, we were ready for our beds.

We also had a battle platoon of specially picked men – I think ten in number. Two or three were picked from each several village. The battle platoon could be called upon to help any other platoon that was in trouble. One evening about nine o'clock, while it was raining hard, Kimbolton Castle was being 'attacked' and we were called on to reinforce the defending platoon.

Our platoon was entered in a competition. Four platoons were to attack a certain target. One Sunday morning, the target was near Northampton and the competition was being watched by a regular army colonel and there were four Northampton umpires. The commanding officers of the four platoons each drew a ticket out of a hat and we were first to go. When we finished our attack on the target, we were lined up in front of the colonel. He made a speech about our performance and said it was excellent – as good as any regular army platoon could have done – and that whoever beat it would have to be perfect. The four umpires recorded the points scored. Then two of the other platoons performed and had their points recorded, and finally the Northampton platoon performed. When the points were all counted up, the Northampton platoon had beaten us by one point – but, as all the umpires came from Northampton, that was no surprise to us! But we were well satisfied with the result.

On another Sunday morning, our whole platoon combined with the Yelling platoon and made an attack on Molesworth Airfield. As we closed in on the airfield, we could hear the bullets buzzing over our heads, so I asked the first black Yank we came to, "Are you using live ammunition?" He said, "Yes, but we are shooting mighty high." But some of those bullets didn't seem very high to me!

We were lucky, all being issued with Lee Enfield rifles. I know lots of Home Guard members had to train with broomsticks. We had a regular army sergeant major to train us with our weapons. I started with a 303 rifle, then they were all called in and replaced with 300s. I did training with a cup-discharger, then I was issued with a Sten gun.

To use the cup-discharger, I used blank ammunition. I turned my rifle upside-down, standing the butt on the ground. Then I got a Mill's hand-grenade, removed the pin, holding the clip down, and slid the grenade into the tight-fitting cup on the end of the barrel. I took my aim from the long sight fixed halfway down the barrel and fired. The blank cartridge threw the grenade several hundred yards.

We were also trained to put oil on the roads to disable motorbikes and we also put steel wire across the roads at the right height to catch the motor-cyclists under the chin. We were also taught unarmed combat and field-craft – but most of us didn't need much field-craft training, as we had been brought up in the fields.

When we were patrolling the roads at night, our orders were to stop everyone we saw and ask to see their indentity cards. When we were patrolling the bridges, we often found tramps sleeping under the archways. Our orders were to turn them out, which caused a lot of unpleasantness.

One night, around midnight, I went under the archway at Great Paxton and, as I shone my torch under the bridge, I saw four heaps of hay, so I kicked one heap of hay – and kicked someone underneath it. He started to swear when I told him, "You will have to get out of here." He refused to go, so I said, "You will get out – or have a hole through you." He said, "Don't shoot – I will go." Then I kicked the other three heaps over, and found three more blokes under them. There was a lot more swearing when I told them they had to get out, but they all went in the end.

During the 1944 harvest, I contracted to swob a field of peas for Mr Tom Chapman on Monks Hardwicke Farm. As I was cutting the peas, I cut over several objects which had their tops sticking out of the ground. The biggest part of them was buried in the ground – and I thought they looked like incendiary bombs. I went and told Mr Chapman and he and his son, Jack, came to have a look at the objects. They agreed with me and went home and rung the Police, who got in touch with the Bomb Squad, who came out and collected the incendiary bombs.

I came across a lot of those bombs, scattered about the fields. When Jerry dropped them, they came out of what was called a 'bread-basket', which contained a hundred or two. The light from them, as they dropped, was a brilliant white and we could see for miles around.

When I was walking across one of Mr Chapman's fields, I saw a large round hole in the ground and thought it must be a bomb. I told Mr Chapman, who got in touch with the Bomb Squad. They came to have a look and, the next day, four men came with a digger and dug a hole about 16 feet square, all around the bomb. On the Friday afternoon, I went to see how they were getting on. They had just finished digging and there was the old bomb, a 1000-pounder, standing upright in the middle of the hole – about 15 feet deep. It was a sight I shall never forget. The next morning, about 11 o'clock, I was walking along the park at Monks Hardwicke with my gun and dog, shooting rabbits, when that bomb exploded. I thought it had burst my eardrums.

One night Yelling and Toseland Home Guard were 'attacking' Papworth Colony. As we were surrounding Papworth Village, we could see the glow over London and the flashing of the bombs as it suffered a particularly heavy blitz. We could also see the sparks from the Ack-Ack gun shells quite plainly.

My son, Ray, and I were standing outside our house one afternoon and saw a German bomber dropping bombs on the Little Barford power station. Then it came along towards Great Paxton, machine-gunning a train as it travelled along. One Saturday afternoon, we also saw the plane that dropped the bombs on Papworth St Agnes.

I also remember when we went to Yarmouth for a day's outing and saw the Graf Zeppelin – not far out, over the sea.

On the night the Germans bombed Coventry, we were on Home Guard duty. It seemed as if the planes were coming over us for hours. We could recognise the droning noise of the old German engines – they had a different sound to our planes and It was just the same when the Germans bombed Manchester. And they would often drop an odd bomb anywhere on their way home.

One night when Jerry came over, he dropped hundreds of Butterfly bombs, which lay on the ground until something – or someone – touched them, when they would explode. A lot of them fell in Mr John Manning's field of sanfoin, near the Toseland crossroads. The police walked about nearly all the next day in the sanfoin, looking for the bombs as the crop was ready to cut. It would be very dangerous if they were hit by the cutter!

Quite a lot of them fell in Mr Arthur Topham's field along Graveley Road, also in Ron Hedge's field on the corner of Graveley Road and Yelling Road and in Mr Farr's field opposite where the old windmill stood. In the old mill yard, there still stands a small building which, during the First World War, was full of bombs and had sandbags built up all around it. It is now an Historic Building.

On Christmas afternoon in 1944, it was very foggy. I went along to

Lodge Farm, to Mr and Mrs Livett's, where we played darts. Their son, Reg, went outside and, when he came back into the house, he told us he had heard what sounded like shots in the direction of Great Paxton, so we all went outside to listen. I thought a plane had crashed, so Reg Livett and I jumped on our bikes and went to London Lane, Great Paxton, where we found a Lancaster bomber which had crashed. It had taken off from number one runway at Graveley Airfield. It banked too soon and took the tops off some young trees, which pulled the plane round into Great Paxton village. The wing of the plane had ripped the tiles off four council houses before it crashed into the garden of another council house, where Stanley Jackson was feeding his hens. He saw the bomber coming through the dense fog and ran into his house. After the plane crashed, he found that all the hens he had been feeding had been killed. When Reg and I arrived, the first thing we saw was a huge Australian chap, just inside the cricket field, with his head split open. He was quite dead. George Carrol had just pulled another chap out of the wreckage – he was just alive, but the others were all killed. The bombs that the plane carried were strewn in all directions.

One night, when the siren had sounded, I looked out of my bedroom window and saw a German bomber, picked out by several of our searchlights. I had a lovely view, as it was not very high. The bomber was going towards Diddington and the only searchlight that kept on it was the one from Diddington. When the bomber was directly above the searchlight, I heard four bombs explode - and the searchlight went out.

One night, about midnight, Ron Beal and I were on Home Guard duty. On our way home, someone came along on a bicycle, so I stopped him. It was P.C. Millard, who lived at Graveley, and had just left St Neots Police Station. He told me, "Not tonight. There were no enemy planes crossing the coast tonight." But I was sure I had heard one. "I dare bet any money that there was a Jerry," I said. He said, "There hasn't been a yellow [warning] light tonight, let alone a red." As he said that four bombs dropped at Swineshead and, in a few seconds, six more fell in the grass meadow close to Mr Joey Robert's farm and cottages, near the corner where the Abbotsley road leaves the Potton road. P.C. Millard said, "That's funny, we haven't had any notice at all tonight about enemy action."

During both world wars, there were some very sad times, but we also had some happy times. When I went into pubs for a drink, I met servicemen from other countries. The piano would be playing and nearly everyone would be singing all the old songs and enjoying themselves. On Christmas Eve, we sang Christmas carols. A week before Christmas, children came round the houses singing carols – and hoping to get a few coppers to spend for Christmas – that gave everybody a 'Christmas feeling' All that has died out now. Nowadays, the pub on Christmas Eve is just like any other evening – no carol singing and no 'Christmas spirit'.

During the Second World War, when I was contracting for War Agricultural work and employed 20 men; if any man wanted a pair of wellingtons, I had to get a special permit for them. There were also special permits for bread, cheese, butter and tea, because the work they were doing was very physical labour and extra food was necessary. There was also petrol rationing, so coupons were necessary for that.

For a good many years (around 1947), my wife Hilda and I went to the pictures twice a week in St Neots – on Wednesdays and Saturdays. We booked our seats each Saturday for the next week, both days, so we had the same seats every time we went – they were reserved for us. We went in all weathers. If there was deep snow, we walked to St Neots; but whenever the weather was suitable, we cycled. We went in the afternoon, did our shopping and left it with Mr and Mrs Hunt, the butchers in Huntingdon Street, where we left our cycles. Then off we went for tea at the Priory Restaurant (which is now Tooks), then to the pictures. When the pictures ended, out we came and Mrs Hunt would often have supper ready for us before we cycled home.

One Saturday afternoon, my wife and I went to St Neots for some shopping in our Vauxhall car. Just as we got to Huntingdon Street, we ran into water on the road. I kept going until we reached East Street. We couldn't go any further as the water was too deep. We saw a big tank with some folk standing on top of it handing food to people through their bedroom windows. So I turned the car round and went back home without the shopping.

While I was contracting for agriculture work in 1950, my wife, my son, Ray, and I were digging a main drain at Guilden Morden, when an old chap came to us. He said, "When you get up about another hundred yards, you will cut through a bush drain that we put in seventy years ago. We cut a big hedge down and put in a drain and I am eager to see what the wood is like now, after seventy years". When we got to that drain, we had to use an axe to cut through the wood, as it was harder that the day it was put on. The old chap could hardly believe his eyes and said he didn't think he would ever see that wood again, and was very pleased to do so.

In 1954, we went to Waresley to play cricket. Mr Charles Banks said, "Hello, so you have come to see us again. I have got my son Sidney turning out today for the first time. He is hoping to make a fast bowler." "That's good news," I said, "I hope he does." We won the toss and batted first. I opened the batting and carried my bat through the innings for 69, not out, out of the score of 111 runs. As we left the field, Mr Charles Banks patted me on the shoulder and said, "Congratulations, young man, you have carried your bat through, haven't you?" I said, "Yes." "That's a thing I shall never do," he said. "I should never have the patience." Then he said, "My son didn't make much impression today." I said, "Your son bowled well, Mr Banks, he got three wickets." But Mr Banks replied, "But he didn't get yours, did he?" We had an easy win that day.

I carried my bat through for five runs against Great Paxton at Toseland. We scored eight runs. I scored five, Fred Peak scored one and there were two extras - eight in all.

I went to play for Hilton at Fen Drayton Feast and we batted first. We scored 11 runs. I carried my bat through the innings for five. Mr Fred Furness came in and he hit his first ball out of the field for six – and was clean bowled next ball! That was the score – 11 and nine ducks!

In later years, a sports club was formed at Mr Harley's. I was captain of the cricket team. I remember one match, when St Ives were playing at Paxton Hill on Mr Harley's ground. I was not playing in that match but I remember our team scored 29 and my son Ray carried his bat through the innings for 25 out of the 29.

We had some very enjoyable games at Mr Harley's ground. When it finished, my son Ray joined St Neots Club. He was opening bat for 12 years and played a number of times for the county team. One year, while he was playing for St Neots, he finished the season with an average of 51.

While I was contracting for agricultural work, we did work all over Cambridgeshire and as far afield as West Wickham, where we laid a lot of pipe behind the old Fordson Digger and the Buck-Eye. For several years, my wife, son and I laid pipes – mostly four-inch ones – behind those two machines. My wife worked with us full time and was as good as most men. When she was working for Mr Roy Anthony on the land outside our house, Mr Anthony was talking to someone and I heard him say, "The best man I have working for me is a woman!" My wife, Hilda, was brought up to hard work, working for her father on his smallholding. We all three liked hard work – the rougher the job, the better we liked it – and we always took pride in our work.

We were on a very rough job one day – cutting bushes that had grown over a big brook – blackberry briars and all sorts of stuff. A man came to us and said, "You folk are gluttons for work, aren't you? Not many folk would tackle a job like that by hand."

Many a time I have taken on the job of sowing top dressing with fertilizer, all by hand, on the corn. We used to sow two hundredweights to the acre. We had a bucket each and a piece of rope tied to the bucket to put round our necks. One day, I had nine men sowing the fertilizer and we were all going along, side by side. The foreman came along and said, "I am looking for the one who is letting the fertilizer trickle out of his bucket." While he was looking about, the stuff we were sowing happened to be a bit lumpy, so my son, Ray, slung a lump and hit the foreman beside the earhole! He didn't look any more and got out of the way as quickly as he could. That was a tiring old job, carrying a bucket of fertilizer all day. Now things have changed today, when one man sitting in a tractor cab can get over 100 acres or more a day.

Years ago, nearly all the crops had to be horse-hoed or hoed by hand to kill the weeds. When he was hand hoeing, a man would take four rows at a time. If he was horse-hoeing, he would take eight rows at a time. When the beans were horse-hoed, he would take one full row and one half row – with the half rows on the outside. Nowadays weeds are killed by spraying.

While I was contracting, my son, Ray, was called up into the Air Force, in the middle of harvest, which made things a bit awkward, as he was running one harvest gang and I was running the other.

Ray flew out from Waterbeach to Burma and, when he arrived there, his pest-controlling skills came in very handy. They were billeted close to Rangoon Docks with 56 F.R.U. (Forward Repair Unit). The buildings that had been bombed there were alive with rats. The rats were darker than ours in England and a bit smaller. As the men lay on their bunks at night, they could see 20 or 30 rats running along the beams above them. Ray said to his mates, "I will see if I can put a stop to some of these." So he got some wire netting and wrapped it round a chair. Then he made a funnel each side, put some cheese inside and placed the chair in the spare room, next to his mate. Next morning the 'char-waller' and his mate came and said, "There is a lot of squealing going on in the spare room." They went to have a look and, to Ray's delight, the 'cage' was full of rats. There were 19 in the cage, so they rang the first officer (who was a Warrant Officer) and he was very excited when he saw the rats. He asked Ray to go down to the carpenter's shop, to show them how to build the cages. Ray had to go down every day to put funnels on the cages. Then he took the cages to the officers' quarters and placed them on tables beside the officers' beds. The rats were eating the officers' soap and chocolate! Some cages were also placed on the cookhouse floor and Ray told me that hundreds of rats were caught in cages there.

Then my son was moved to 55 M.T.C. (Motor Transport Company), where he played in four football matches every week. Then, after a while, he was moved from Rangoon to Calcutta, where he played a lot of cricket. He went to many other parts of the world, including Italy, Egypt and Palestine. That was an experience he will never forget. Then I got him out of the Air Force to come and work for me. He came home on the liner, *The Duchess of Bedford*. He carried on where he left off – doing a lot of hard graft, tree felling.

Ray turned out to be a great sportsman, playing football, cricket, shooting and fishing. He was captain of the Blue Bell Darts Team at Toseland. He was also interested in self-defence, and was mad on flying. Most Saturdays, when he was in the A.T.C. (Air Training Corps), he would go up in Lancasters and Halifaxes from Graveley, and with the Yanks in the Flying Fortresses from Staughton Airfield.

As the farms became more mechanised, the contract jobs died out, so we turned to growing our own Brussels sprouts for five or six years. The brussel trade was always best when the weather was rough, with frost and snow. Many a time we have left home in the morning when it had been snowing, smothering the brussels and, when we got into the field, we couldn't see the brussels for snow. We swept away the snow from the brussel stalks with our feet before we could pick the sprouts.

Some people wore gloves for brussel picking, but I never did. I was never troubled with cold hands. I earned every penny I got at that job but I used to love it, even though, when I had my meals, I had to sit out in the middle of the fields to eat them. My eyelids would often stick together with the frost. One thing we used to do when brusseling was to leave a good picking for the Christmas Market. Many a time we have been picking sprouts in the moonlight. At Christmas, most of the salesmen would send down a box of oranges, apples or bananas for the pickers. One day, Ray picked 140 nets of brussels, while picking for Ronald Hedge of Toseland. That was a good day's work.

During the sharp winter of 1963, when my son was picking brussels for Mr Harley, he had to kick the sprouts off and then pick them up. I stood in the flight line in one corner of the field, where the pigeons were coming to the brussels and had a great big fire every day. I shot and shot until I had a very sore finger from what the trigger guard had done, so then I couldn't fire my gun. The pigeons came to the brussels in hundreds, so I had a stick and walked among the brussels, knocking the pigeons with my stick - they were too weak to fly. A lot of small birds lay among the brussels, frozen to death.

I often think how lucky I was to have a gang of men working for me right through the war, and, for a while, after the war was over. My gang of men were as follows:

Harold Meeks (myself)	Bob Horner
Walter Meeks (my father)	Sam Hedge
Buller Meeks	Perce Reed

Reg Meeks	Bert Sanford
Charlie Norman	Charlie Dawborn
Billy Hickman	King Mitchell
Gordon Revell	Bill Cook
Sid Hills	Art Baker
Dennis Meeks	Joe Currington
Ray Meeks (my son)	Owen Currington
Frank Tack	

I often think of the good times we had together – they were hard days, but happy. Ray and I often visit Dumptilow Farm, which is now farmed by Mr Sperling. That is where I started my contract work. When we go into the old building up there, it certainly brings back memories. When we were there during the war, and there was a wet day, we used to go into the building, stick a knife in the floor and play pitch-halfpenny!

Left This photograph was taken in Russia in 1880. It shows Harold's wife's mother and grandmother. The grandmother was a Russian countess.

Below Harold and Hilda's wedding – 26th March 1924

Back row (left to right) George Leach, Mary Hickman (aunt), Jess Meeks (uncle), Mabel Meeks (cousin), Bridesmaid from Luton, Harold Meeks, Hilda Meeks, Buller Meeks (Bestman and brother), Margaret Meeks, Arthur Meeks (brother), Mrs Leach, Reginald Meeks (brother).

Front row Stanley Meeks (brother), Violet Currington (sister), Haddon Currington (nephew), Walter Meeks (father), Alfred Topham (father in law), Nellie Meeks (Charlie's wife), Dennis Meeks (nephew), Charlie Meeks.

Photograph taken on Reg's Wedding Day, 20th March 1943
Left to right Reg Meeks, Arthur Meeks, Walter Meeks (father), Charlie Meeks, Violet (father's sister), Buller Meeks and Harold Meeks. The missing brother was Stanley, who was unable to attend.

High Hayden Farm, Yelling

This photograph was lent by Frank Reed. It shows Edward (Ted) Smith driving a caterpillar tractor, John Benham (Jack), George Baxter, Percy Reed (Perce) and the manager Mr Arthur Childerly.

Harold and son in 1927.

Raymond in 1929 with beloved cricket bat and ball. The dog was called Carlo.

Harold and Ray after a days shooting on Mr Steve Mear's clover at Waresley. The photograph was taken by John Clark in 1960. The dog's name was Joyce and they killed 468 pigeons after one o'clock.

Above Harold and Hilda outside their house in 1956, they were just going out for a ride in their Standard Eight car.

Right 17th August 1957

This photograph of Ray, Hilda and Harold was taken outside Toseland church by George Page of St Neots.

3. Reflections

Sometimes, when I think back a bit, I know I must be getting on in years. I did a lot of work for Mr Bill Topham of Eltisley and a lot of work for his sons, George and Ray, and a lot of work for Ray's son, Peter – so I have done work for three generations of Tophams. I would say they are some of the biggest and best farmers in the country.

We were doing some work for Mr Ray Topham when my illness came along. I went into hospital on 20th October 1970 and was operated on on the 22nd October. It was a major operation and I was in Huntingdon County Hospital for nine weeks. I went into hospital again in January 1972 and had two more major operations for a perforated bowel. I was in hospital for 13 weeks and had 15 feet of my bowel removed and my colostomy fixed. In January 1973, I went into hospital again and had two more major operations – and had more bowel removed. I was in hospital that time for 16 weeks. The first operation was done by Mr Everett and the next four by Mr Smellie of Addenbrookes Hospital. Mr Smellie was not keen on doing my last operation alone, as he said I might die, so he had the help of Professor Carne and, as you can see, I pulled through and am still here to tell the tale! One person I have to thank is Sister Payne – she was simply wonderful and is one person I shall never forget.

Now, 20 years after my first operation, I am flat out with my gun every day, pigeon shooting, rabbit catching and also hedge-trimming, which I still love doing. Also, I still drive my car at 92 years old, so I can't grumble. I also enjoy the pigeon shooting and rabbit catching.

How things have changed in the country. I never see anyone working in the fields unless they are on a tractor these days. Years ago, there were many men working in the fields, hedge-trimming, cleaning out ditches, picking brussels and putting up potatoes out of the potato clamps. There were also men with horses ploughing, cultivating, harrowing, rolling and drilling. All the village men worked on the farms. They could be seen digging the corners of the fields, close to the hedgerows, so they cultivated every inch of ground they could get.

Now there are thousands of acres what they call 'set-aside' – growing nothing but rubbish, which doesn't make much sense to me. Instead of importing so many vegetables into this country, we could be growing them instead of rubbish.

When I go into a farmyard today, it seems quite dead. When I was a boy, there were horses in the stables and the horse yard and another yard full of bullocks. The milking cows, when they were not in the fields, were in a separate yard. There were styes full of pigs and other pigs running around in the yards. Hens, cockerels and turkeys were scratching about everywhere and there were ducks and geese swimming about on the horse pond.

I often think about when I was a boy, about 80 years ago or more. On a nice summer's evening, several of us kids would be sitting on the road, playing marbles, noughts and crosses, sticks and stones or Tippy Cat. The women from the village would be coming past to go to the allotments to meet their husbands, who had just left their work in the fields. The women were bringing them some food and a can of tea, so that they could do some work in their allotments when they had finished their tea. When they decided they had had enough for one day, we would see them coming home with their baskets full of new potatoes, green beans, broad beans, runner beans, etc. Almost every householder in the village had a piece of land in the allotments – but today that is a thing of the past.

All my schooldays were at Yelling School and I remember going to the Peace celebrations in 1918, when the First World War ended. I hadn't been in that school again until I went to the Christmas Whist Drive in 1988 – after 70 years! Some of the folk, when I told them, asked whether there was anything I could remember about the old school. So I went and pointed to a spot on the wall where the schoolmaster's cane used to hang. I remembered that alright!

I wish I could go back to my cricketing days, of which I enjoyed every minute. I remember when I used to play for St Neots on the Common and the outfield was all cow muck, in which the ball would very often land. The fielder would pick the ball out of the muck and throw it, either at the wicket-keeper or the bowler, without wiping it. If the bowler had rubbed the ball on his trousers in those days, like they do today, their trousers would have been a rare mess! I have seen some bowlers lick the ball these days and then shine it on their trousers. If they had done that in those days in St Neots years ago, I think that would have been rather tasty!

There have been a lot of other changes in the last 20 years. In those days, I have counted more than 300 cars on the Common, and my brother Charlie went round with a collection box and often collected £15 or £16. But today on a Saturday or Sunday, when my son Ray and I go to the Common to watch the cricket, we are very often the only ones there. Although today they have a nice wicket and a lovely outfield with no cow dung or stinging nettles (in which we often lost the ball) the standard of cricket has fallen away quite a lot. Twenty or 25 years ago, each town in the county had a very strong team – there was St Neots, St Ives, Huntingdon, Ramsey and Warboys; whenever any two of these teams met it was always a real 'Derby'. I must also include the Huntingdonshire Police, who had a very strong side. The cricket improved quite a lot in the county at the time when the England fast bowler Nobby Clarke left Northampton and took over the Dun Horse public house at St Ives. The opening attacks were far different in those days with Nobby Clarke and Reg Presland for St Ives, Jim Gambrel and Fagg for Huntingdon, Tony Lavender and Foster for Ramsey – and Sid Eayrs was another good opening bowler for Warboys.

One year, in the Smith Barry Final between Huntingdon and St Neots, it seemed certain that Huntingdon would win, when St Neots' last man came in to bat with his side needing over 100 runs to win – but they got them and won the Cup. Vic Davies scored 101 not out and won the Jack Hobbs Bat; Dick Sillet held his wicket up while Vic Davies did the scoring.

On another occasion, when St Neots beat Huntingdon in the Smith Barry Final, my son Ray and Dennis Barnett opened the batting for St Neots. That day, Kenny Pateman was almost unplayable and took most of the wickets. The game was played at Warboys and the interest was so keen that it was a job to find a parking space for my car anywhere round the ground so I could watch the game. The shouting and cheering was almost deafening.

I always looked forward to Eltisley Feast week, when I would be playing cricket every day of the week for different teams. One Saturday, when I was playing for Caxton, I was running up the pitch, when my foot broke through the ground onto a nest of young rabbits. I wondered what was up!

One Saturday evening, over 70 years ago, I went into The Two Brewers public house in St Neots and sat talking to a man. He said, "You are playing St Neots next Saturday at Yelling, aren't you?" I told him that I was. "Well," said he,"I can tell you how you are going to get out." He had heard some of the St Neots players talking in the pub that night. They were talking to the umpire about how to get me out. The umpire said to one of the bowlers, "If you can hit his legs and appeal, I will give him out, whether he is front of the wicket, or not." The man said, "So now you know."

I also remember one day when a bowler appealed to the umpire for L.B.W. and the umpire said, "Not out - but, if he does it again, he will be out!"

My brother Charlie told me about Eltisley cricket team getting knocked out by St Neots for one run – and that was when Eltisley had got a good team. Old Simon Maddy took the wickets.

I remember Croxton cricket team coming to Yelling and, when the last man came into to bat for Croxton, they had scored only three runs. Jess Saywell came in last and scored three twos, which took their score to nine. Part of the reason for their low scores was the rough wickets and the outfield was long mowing grass, all round the wickets. To score runs, we had to hit the ball up in the air and there was every chance of being caught out. I can honestly say that bowling 60 or 70 years ago was quicker than anything I see today. Every village had two or three really fast bowlers but, in those days, I never saw a batsman wearing chest pads, thigh pads, arm pads or even a box like they do today. Some batsmen went in to bat with one pad on the front leg – and no batting gloves.

I was an opening bat all my cricketing life, for 40 years. I opened the innings for Yelling when I was 13 years old and I was still opening bat when I finished at age 53. My brother Buller opened the batting with me for Yelling for a good many years. When I played for St

Neots in the Tuesday Team whith Ernie Albone as captain, I always opened with Frank Rawlings, the Bedfordshire opening bat and wicket-keeper, or Claude Lovitt, who was a very good bat.

The Meeks family have always been a real cricketing family, so my son Ray has followed in my footsteps as opening bat. All his cricketing life, wherever he played and whoever he played for, he has always opened the innings. My nephew, Geoffrey Meeks – my brother Buller's son – also opened for Eltisley for a good many years, in fact all his cricketing life. My sister Violet's son, Haddon Currington, also played cricket for Yelling and, later, for Great Gransden.

My cousin, Bill Smith, of Eaton Socon, went in for a different kind of sport – if you can call it sport! I think it was jolly hard work! It was bicycle racing, at which he was an expert. Unfortunately, he has recently died but, on Sunday 25th March 1990, my son and I visited his wife and she showed us the trophies he won for cycle racing. He won the 25-miles road race, the 50-miles and the 100-miles, which I consider was jolly good going. He has left behind his wife, his son Roger of Eaton Socon, who is a very good clay pigeon shot and a daughter Diana, who lives at Leicester. Bill was a first-class carpenter. Before he retired, he was manager at Gullifords the builders. Bill Smith married Miss Joan Thody of Graveley during the Second World War and I was best man at their wedding. We spent many happy times together.

Bill's father, Bill Smith senior, also of Eaton Socon used to drive Jordan and Addingtons Foden Waggon for some years. He was a very strong man and could take hold of a sack of corn by the mouth of the sack and swing it about as if it was chaff. He carried five sacks of wheat, each weighing 18 stones four pounds from one end of Jordan and Addington's mill to the other – two on his shoulders, one on top of the other and three on a sack barrow.

There is no bodily work on farms now – all the corn today is moved in bulk. Years ago, when the corn stacks were threshed, the corn was weighed at the drum into sacks. Oats weighed up at 12 stones, barley at 16 stones, wheat at 18 stones, peas and beans at 19 stones and clover at 20 stones. How much everything has changed.

I didn't think I should live to see the day when St Neots town hadn't got a football team. Years ago, they had quite a good team and it was always a local 'Derby' when they played Eynesbury Rovers, as Eynesbury had a good side too. They used to draw a very large crowd of spectators. In St Neots, there were the town team, the town reserves, the St Mary's and the Wesleyans — now it all seems like a dream, as they are all finished and the Shortsands football ground closed down — what a shame!

In my younger days, I was very fond of football and, for several years, I played for the Yelling team, then the Toseland team, then we combined and played at Croxton — we had a very useful side. Many a time, after we had been out shooting all Saturday morning, walking the ploughed fields, we hurried home and changed into our football clothes, putting our trousers and jacket over the top of them. We hadn't got time for any dinner, so we hurried off to wherever we were playing, took off our top clothes (jacket, trousers, etc.) and laid them on the ground under a tree or near a hedge. If it had been raining while we were playing, we had to put on our soaking wet clothes and cycle home.

I remember watching St Ives playing football at St Neots — when St Neots football ground was on the left, coming out of St Neots, towards Great Paxton, somewhere near the Crescent. There was a Mr Smith, a schoolmaster, who I think played centre forward; but he was a very big man and didn't run about much, and just waited for the passes to come to him. He was a left-foot kick and one day he got a pass and took a mighty kick, which broke the crossbar. I was standing near some St Ives spectators and heard them say, "That is three he has broken this year." I had never seen anyone kick so hard in my life.

My youngest brother's grandson, Anthony Meeks, son of Brian Meeks, looks as if he is a very promising footballer. At the age of 14, he was on the Tottenham Hotspurs' books quite a while but now he is on Luton Town's books, as it is closer for training.

The first sugar-beet grown in this country was at Mr Knight's 24 acres. Two or three Germans came over from Germany to supervise. I was one of 16 who did the setting out. We all had so many rows alloted to us. None of us had seen any of this work before. When we had been working for about an hour, Mr Knight and the Germans came and inspected every man's work. I was in the middle (and I'm not bragging) and, when they got to me, one of the Germans said to Mr Knight, "This young man is doing a first class job – that is exactly how we would like the job done." Then they went right down the field and looked at the work of all the other men. Then they brought the other men up to my work and Mr Knight said to them, "Now, you chaps, Harold is the youngest one here and he is doing the job better than any man in the field." And the Germans agreed, saying, "That is exactly how we would like the job to be done." As they were leaving, Mr Knight said to me, "We shall have to give you a hundredweight of sugar, boy, when we harvest the beet." He always called me 'boy.' Mr Knight was a very nice man.

Now I will tell you about pigeon shooting over decoys. A decoy is a pigeon that is put out on a field to draw the live ones, so they can be shot. Some people use dead ones and some people use artificial ones – but we preferred dead ones. I have been shooting pigeons over decoys for nearly 80 years – and I am still doing it to this day. I have studied pigeons since I was eight years old, when I went with my father and also my uncle. If they went to pick up a pigeon which was some distance away, and a pigeon came into the decoys, although I was only eight years old, I would pick up a gun and have a go. I have studied their movements, their feeding sites, feeding times and flight lines. Sixty or seventy years ago there were only one or two pigeon-shooters in the village. They were called 'Lone Wolves'. Nobody came from the towns to shoot pigeons. Then I could pick my day for shooting – because you can be one day too soon or one day too late. But you can't do that today as there are so many pigeon-shooters who come out of the towns. They don't know the first thing about the job and just spoil a good day's shooting.

In 1989, Joe Townsend of Great Paxton came to my house and told me that his field of wheat, along the brook, was flat to the ground and covered with pigeons. He asked me to come and have a go at them. "You will want a lot of cartridges," he said. I agreed to go right away. When I got to the field, I found Mr Jack Rampley, the farmer from Little Paxton, was there. He was a real old pigeon shooter and asked if I was going to have a go at the pigeons. I told him that Mr Townsend had been along to my house to ask me to come. Mr Rampley said, "You go to the other end of the field and I will stay this end." So away I went to the other end of the field, made my hide and put out my decoys. As soon as I was in my hide, the pigeons started to come. Mr Rampley was in their flight-path and had the first go at them. I could see he was missing a lot and they were coming straight along to me and I was fetching them down as fast as they came. I had got a large heap in my hide when we packed up. Mr Rampley came along to me and said, "Well, boy, you have shown me the way to shoot pigeons today. I have been classed as 'Pigeon King' of this area for a good many years, but today you have taken the title from me. From now on, **you** are 'Pigeon King'." I have spent a lot of my life in a pigeon hide and enjoyed it. I would rather be in a hide, waiting for pigeons, than going for a day at the sea.

When I am sitting in a hide, waiting for pigeons, it is surprising what I see and notice. In 1989, I was sitting on my shooting stick in a hide, when a rabbit came into the hide and sat there for about ten minutes. During that time, it sniffed the ground, then started scratching, then sniffed again, then scratched again – it was very amusing to watch, as it was only about a yard away from me.

I have also read a lot of articles in different books about how to place the decoys – and their ideas are far different from mine! My son Ray and I always place our decoys to look as natural as possible, and on different feeding sites. We put our decoys in different positions, not in line, like soldiers on parade, or in other patterns, or with a space left as a killing ground. For 80 years at the job, I have never seen pigeons feeding to a pattern, and, as for a space for a killing ground, anywhere is a killing ground for my son and me, as soon as the pigeons get within shooting distance. We have killed hundreds of thousands and worn out six guns. During my working days, my son and I averaged over 10,000 pigeons every year, and, in 1981, we killed 18,037 in seven months, from the beginning of October to the end of April.

On two occasions, we have passed 600 pigeons in one day and seven times, we had over 500, and many times we had more than 400. Some years ago, if we didn't come home with at least 200, we thought we had had a bad day. I remember one day standing in a ditch, waiting for pigeons, when two came over at great speed in a very strong wind.

I fired at both birds and they both folded up. But, as they were travelling so fast, they carried on for about 100 yards, where there were three electricity wires. Both pigeons hit those wires, which cut them both in half - so I picked up four halves, and they were useless.

The decline of the hare is mentioned in a number of magazines. One reason for this is lamping at night, with bright lights on vehicles which dazzle the hares so they will sit and be shot. If this is allowed to go on for a few more years, the hare will be extinct. I have been a shooting man for over 80 years, but I have never done that kind of shooting and I am I sure I never shall. I think it is the lowest and most unsporting grade of shooting that anyone can do. A few years ago, that kind of shooting would never have been allowed and not even thought about.

When I was a lad, on the first day of September, big partridge shoots took place and hundreds of partridges were killed and a large number of hares and rabbits would be sitting about in the stubbles and in potatoes, or mangolds, or in a bunch of long grass and anywhere there was a bit of cover.

A Graveley man, named Fred Tack (Otty) was working for Mr Farr on Manor Farm, Yelling, when I was working there. One morning he was coming to work down the old bridle road after snow had fallen a couple of days before. The snow was frozen hard and Fred saw a hole in the snow. He took off his big overcoat and threw it over the hole not knowing what was in it. When he looked under the coat, he saw a lot of partridges, which he killed one by one. When he had finished he had 16 lovely partridges – all English. That was in about 1914, but I must say that the partridge population was very different in those days.

I used to see rabbits sitting in forms but now I scarcely ever see a rabbit sitting in a form and no partridges and very few hares to shoot. There are very few shoots where there are only wild pheasants to be shot, as most birds are reared; but there is one estate in this area where all the birds are wild birds and provide some very good shooting. That estate belongs to Mr Sperling of Papworth St Agnes.

Thinking about the Sperlings' estate reminds me that, in 1921, my father and I were going along the brook in Barnfield Lane to do some rabbit catching. My father was getting over a stile, close to the old footbridge. It was a frosty morning and the post, which was placed there to take hold of to help a person to get over the stile, was very slippery at the top. My father's hand slipped off and let his body fall on to the post. It broke three of his ribs and he had to walk back to Yelling. A nasty experience.

My son and I did the gamekeeping for Mr Harley of the Aircraft Landing lights, though there were only hedgerows and no woods – and only two fields wide. When the shooting season commenced, my son and I did the shooting for Mr and Mrs Harley and were joined by Mr Alec Bidwell. Our three guns would kill anything up to 130 pheasants, Saturday after Saturday, as well as partridges, hares and rabbits. Now that has all changed, with the removal of the trees and hedgerows – and the beauty of the coutryside.

I often sit and think about my memories of 90 years, most of which have been spent in the woods or fields. I spent most of my happy days at rabbit catching. In 1919 and 1920, I helped to kill over twenty thousand rabbits each year and, in 1921, my brother Charlie and I killed nearly another nine thousand for Mr Sperling at Papworth St Agnes. In Graveley rough fields up to fifteen hundred rabbits a day were shot.

The change in farming methods and different crops is the reason why there are not so many pigeons killed today as there were years ago.

Another thing I must mention is about a right and left at woodcock, which is talked about a lot today but very seldom happens, whereas, when my son and I used to walk through Graveley rough fields, which held a lot of woodcock, we very often got a right and left at them and thought nothing of it.

Another thing I enjoy very much is going out at the weekends for a drink and a game of dominoes. Sometimes my son and I go to The Spread Eagle at Croxton, as there is no public house in Toseland. There used to be two – The Blue Ball and The Hand in Hand. Sometimes we go to the club at Yelling, which used to be the school for Yelling and Toseland children. I sit to play dominoes at the very spot where I sat 86 years ago when I started school.

Although I have been to The Spread Eagle at Croxton for between 70 and 80 years, going to Yelling now and again makes a change and I enjoy getting among some of the old-timers whom I have known all their lives. We talk about old times and things that happened in the village where I was born. Most of the old ones that I knew quite well and was brought up with have passed on, but a few of them still remain, such as Joe Revell and the Reed and Brook families.

In our small village of Toseland, some years ago, when there were twice the number of people than there are today, I knew every one; but today with only about 70 or 80 people in the village, I don't know half.

Years ago, Toseland was a nice quiet peaceful little village with its two pubs, where we could have a nice quiet drink. Those who didn't drink had got the Reading Room to go to and pass the evening away playing games. Now, the two pubs have gone, there is no shop, no Post Office, nothing. If you want anything, you have got to go into St Neots – or to Mr Thody's at Graveley. No callers come into the village today as they used to. As for being quiet, there is more traffic coming through Toseland today than there was on the A45 a few years ago. If the old people of Toseland could come back to life again and see a car outside almost every house, they would soon go back!

When I am travelling along the road, I glance across the fields – and I can see for miles and miles. But all I can see is the great asbestos buildings. Years ago, I saw corn stacks, straw stacks and the old thatched or tiled buildings, which I am quite sure looked much nicer. I am sorry to say that I'm afraid the beauty of the countryside has gone for ever, never to return. There is so much interference today with country life and country ways.

Now I bring my book to a close with the best wishes for all my readers. I hope they have had as much pleasure in reading it as I have had in writing it. What I have written in my book are my own views and opinions, and I hope I have not offended anyone.

This photograph was taken on Mr Richard Hart's land at Crows-Nest Farm, Papworth on Christmas Eve in 1986. The bag amounted to 604 pigeons on a field of oil-seed rape.

Harold drove Ray to the field at seven o'clock in the morning where they made a hide (behind Harold). He left his gun and cartridges there while he went on to St Neots. When he returned at one o'clock, he found Ray had shot 400 pigeons – and used all of Harold's cartridges as well as his own! Mr Hart was a cartridge dealer; he heard Ray shooting so he took him another 500 cartridges in his Land Rover.

When Harold arrived, he and his son stood side by side and finished the day with 604 pigeons, which they put into plastic sacks and loaded into Mr Hart's Land Rover. They were very thankful that he carried their bag home for them.

Days like that do not happen very often, this was only the second time that Harold and Ray had shot a bag of over 600.

This photograph was taken at Hamerton in 1987. Harold and Ray had put down 80 snares one afternoon. Next morning they picked up 54 rabbits – which Harold considers pretty good going.

Rabbiting on Mr Martin Eayres land at Hamerton in 1987. Harold and Ray have just taken the rabbits out of the snares and are 'legging' them.

This photograph was taken at the Old Cotton's Farm on Graveley Airfield in July 1987.

It was alive with rats where the pheasants were being fed. The chaps who were rearing the pheasants kept putting poison down, but this wasn't checking them. They asked if Harold and Ray could help. They put down some snares, and in five nights caught 85 great big rats – they can be seen hanging in the snares. It may be an old method of pest control, but it is a very good one, says Harold!

   Mr William Topham of Eltisley and Harold.

Mr Topham went to see Harold, because a fox had been on his lawn and killed his lovely old swan, and a duck sitting hard and some chickens. Harold caught the fox on the first night and Mr Topham said it was the largest fox he had ever seen, so he asked his housekeeper to bring her camera and take this photograph of them.

Above Harold and Ray outside Gremblin Grange, the house they had lived in for 57 years. The photograph was taken by Mrs Tossil from the Blue Boar Public House in Toseland in 1987.

Below Harold in his flower garden in 1987. The photograph was taken by Miss Elaine Donaldson of St Neots. She had made a special journey to come and see his sweet peas. (Harold has looked after the hedge at the home of Mrs and Miss Donaldson at St Neots for the last 10 years).

KING'S MUSIC Gmc
Clifford Bartlett
Elaine Bartlett

Redcroft, Banks End, Wyton, Huntingdon, Cambs PE17 2AA   telephone (0480) 52076

Local History — Huntingdonshire

From Bombs to Buckets: Brixton to Papworth St. Agnes, 1940-1948 by Dora Tack.
Wyton, 1988. 180pp, illustrated. ISBN 1 871775 00 0   £8.95

Papworth St. Agnes in the 1940s by Dora Tack. *Forthcoming*

****

Bluntisham: a village remembered by Ernest Ward
Wyton, 1989. 76pp, illustrated. ISBN 1 871775 01 9   £5.95

****

Beyond Yesterday: a History of Fenstanton by Jack Dady.
Wyton, 1987. 103pp   £5.00

"All you ever wanted to know about Fenstanton, but didn't dare to ask"   Cambridgeshire Life

****

Hilton, Huntingdonshire by Jack Dady.
Wyton, 1993. 144pp, illustrated. ISBN 1 871775 027   £9.99

****

Legends and Traditions of Huntingdonshire by W.H.Bernard Saunders.
London & Peterborough, 1888.   303pp   £7.00

A fascinating collections of stories – glimpses into Huntingdonshire life as it was or as our 18th & 19th century predecessors liked to think that it was. Reproduced slightly reduced in size and reformatted to keep the price as low as possible.

****

The History of Godmanchester by Robert Fox.
London, 1831.   391 + xxxxvi pp.   £10.00

This is the standard documentary history of Godmanchester. It is reproduced slightly reduced in size and reformatted.

****

Memorials of Godmanchester Reminiscences of F. W. Bird, edited by
W.H.Bernard Saunders. Peterborough, 1911.   112pp   £4.00

Bird was born in 1837; this series of interviews was published in the Peterborough Advertiser and reissued as a separate book with additional information on local musicians. This reprint gives the fullest text from both versions.

****

England. An Intended Guyde for English Travailers Shewing in generall, how far one Citie, & many Shire-Townes in England, are distant from other Together, with the Shires in perticular: and the Chiefe Townes in every of them... Invented & Collected, by John Norden. London, 1625
                                                                    £2.50

The mileage diagrams in AA Handbooks are not a modern idea! This gives a mileage chart for each county. The chart for Huntingdonshire is available separately printed on card for 25p.

****

Huntingdonshire 1830   £2.00

A reproduction of the Huntingdonshire section of Pigot & Co's Directory, which gives a brief description of each town and village and lists those practicing each profession and trade.